SPARKLE & SHINE

108 M.A.N.T.R.A.S TO BRIGHTEN YOUR DAY AND LIGHTEN YOUR WAY

MEG NOCERO

Illustrated by
KIM ANDERSON

Sparkle & Shine: 108 M.A.N.T.R.A.s to Brighten Your Day and Lighten Your Way

Meg Nocero

Published by Butteries & Bliss LLC.

© Meg Nocero 2020

All rights reserved.

First Edition

No part of this book may be reproduced in any form or by any means without prior consent of the publisher, except for brief quotes used in reviews.

Author Photograph: Michelle Citrin

Cover Design and Illustration: Kim Anderson

ISBN: 978-0-578-79002-2

The Heart's Instructions for a Beautiful Year

Keep breathing, you will know peace and anxiety will fade.

Keep loving, you will know joy and will start to let your troubles go.

Keep moving forward, the Angels will protect you.

Keep smiling, it will melt away the pain.

Keep laughing, it is all just an illusion anyway.

Keep dreaming, it's your story - write something amazing!

~Meg

CONTENTS

Dedication — xix
Foreword — xxi

Prologue — 1
Introduction — 3
How To Use This Book — 7
ASK — 9
SECTION I. PAY ATTENTION — 11

1. Magical M.A.N.T.R.A.: I ask to be a charming gardener who plants seeds of love. — 12
2. Magical M.A.N.T.R.A.: I am decisive as I speak my dreams into existence. — 13
3. Magical M.A.N.T.R.A.: I am worthy of love. — 14
   TO MY BUTTERFLIES — 15
4. Magical M.A.N.T.R.A.: If I stay focused, everything will be just fine. — 16
5. Magical M.A.N.T.R.A.: I am enthusiastic about life. — 17
6. Magical M.A.N.T.R.A.: Stay present, no day but today. — 18
7. Magical M.A.N.T.R.A.: I am enough, today I seek ways to tap into my source. — 19
8. Magical M.A.N.T.R.A.: I am happy, magical and magnificent me. — 20
9. Magical M.A.N.T.R.A.: I am at peace, then balance will follow. — 22
10. Magical M.A.N.T.R.A.: I am a co-creator with the universe. — 23
11. Magical M.A.N.T.R.A.: I believe in my unlimited potential. — 24

12. Magical M.A.N.T.R.A.: I will make the day better for another.   25

    TO MY BUTTERFLIES   26

13. Magical M.A.N.T.R.A.: All is well.   27
14. Magical M.A.N.T.R.A.: I am a divine masterpiece.   28
15. Magical M.A.N.T.R.A.: I give myself my own approval.   29
16. Magical M.A.N.T.R.A.: I don't have to figure it all out, just focus on love.   30
17. Magical M.A.N.T.R.A.: I am authentically me.   31
18. Magical M.A.N.T.R.A.: I am a great storyteller.   32
19. Magical M.A.N.T.R.A.: I expect magic and miracles.   33
20. Magical M.A.N.T.R.A.: What God has for me, God has for me.   34
21. Magical M.A.N.T.R.A.: I am dancing with the universe today.   35
22. Magical M.A.N.T.R.A.: Note to self, let sh*t go.   37
23. Magical M.A.N.T.R.A.: I am a work in progress.   39
24. Magical M.A.N.T.R.A.: I am discovering my beauty within.   40
25. Magical M.A.N.T.R.A.: I always believe that something wonderful is about to happen.   41
26. Magical M.A.N.T.R.A.: We've got this!   42

    TO MY BUTTERFLIES   43

27. Magical M.A.N.T.R.A.: I choose to live my life on my terms.   44
28. Magical M.A.N.T.R.A.: Let's keep hope alive.   45
29. Magical M.A.N.T.R.A.: I inspire magic.   46
30. Magical M.A.N.T.R.A.: I smile as a direct achievement.   47
31. Magical M.A.N.T.R.A.: I choose an attitude of gratitude.   48
32. Magical M.A.N.T.R.A.: I obey my soul, from there I bloom with grace.   49

33. Magical M.A.N.T.R.A.: There are no mistakes in my life. — 50
BELIEVE — 51
SECTION II. BE ASTONISHED — 53
34. Magical M.A.N.T.R.A.: I originate from the extraordinary. — 54
35. Magical M.A.N.T.R.A.: Loving myself fully is the best gift. — 55
36. Magical M.A.N.T.R.A.: I am passionate about life and pursue my purpose. — 56
37. Magical M.A.N.T.R.A.: I let my heart speak louder than my head. — 57
TO MY BUTTERFLIES — 59
38. Magical M.A.N.T.R.A.: I run towards what I love. — 60
39. Magical M.A.N.T.R.A.: I move to the magical beat of the universe. — 61
40. Magical M.A.N.T.R.A.: I ask, believe, and receive. — 62
41. Magical M.A.N.T.R.A.: Expect what you want into your life. — 63
42. Magical M.A.N.T.R.A.: I remember I am a teacher and others are watching. — 64
43. Magical M.A.N.T.R.A.: Change is good, transformation even better. — 65
44. Magical M.A.N.T.R.A.: I embrace my shine. — 66
TO MY BUTTERFLIES — 67
45. Magical M.A.N.T.R.A.: I create a plan to fulfill the greatest vision for my life. — 68
46. Magical M.A.N.T.R.A.: I am pure perfection. — 69
47. Magical M.A.N.T.R.A.: I believe that the universe is unfolding exactly as it should. — 70
48. Magical M.A.N.T.R.A.: I believe that I have an obligation to shine. — 71
49. Magical M.A.N.T.R.A.: Forget about who you will follow, how will you lead? — 72
50. Magical M.A.N.T.R.A.: I stand in my beauty and shine. — 73

51. Magical M.A.N.T.R.A.: Success is in the heart of the beholder. ... 74
52. Magical M.A.N.T.R.A.: Today I step into the effortless flow of life. ... 75
53. Magical M.A.N.T.R.A.: I fulfill my greatest potential. ... 76
54. Magical M.A.N.T.R.A.: I set out to enjoy the view. ... 77
55. Magical M.A.N.T.R.A.: I am tethered to pure positive energy. ... 78
56. Magical M.A.N.T.R.A.: I create life's coming attractions in my imagination. ... 79
57. Magical M.A.N.T.R.A.: How I use my voice IS a choice. ... 80
58. Magical M.A.N.T.R.A.: I am a magical treasure hunter. ... 81
59. Magical M.A.N.T.R.A.: I am in the zone. ... 82
60. Magical M.A.N.T.R.A.: I believe in myself. ... 83

TO MY BUTTERFLIES ... 85

61. Magical M.A.N.T.R.A.: I am healing by loving others. ... 86
62. Magical M.A.N.T.R.A.: I am enthusiastic about my journey. ... 88
63. Magical M.A.N.T.R.A.: Remember who you are. ... 89
64. Magical M.A.N.T.R.A.: I am strong, I never know who I am inspiring. ... 90
65. Magical M.A.N.T.R.A.: I follow the divine to embrace love. ... 91
66. Magical M.A.N.T.R.A.: I choose to take care of myself. ... 92

RECEIVE ... 93

SECTION III. TELL ALL ABOUT IT ... 95

67. Magical M.A.N.T.R.A.: I live from an abundance mindset. ... 96
68. Magical M.A.N.T.R.A.: I surrender to joy. ... 97
69. Magical M.A.N.T.R.A.: I embrace simplicity with a K.I.S.S. ... 98

70. Magical M.A.N.T.R.A.: I choose to be a little creatively insane.   99
71. Magical M.A.N.T.R.A.: I give myself permission to dream big.   100
72. Magical M.A.N.T.R.A.: I am a magical creative being.   101

TO MY BUTTERFLIES   103

73. Magical M.A.N.T.R.A.: I show up brave whatever life throws my way.   104
74. Magical M.A.N.T.R.A.: I honor my feelings.   105
75. Magical M.A.N.T.R.A.: I enjoy the magic of my journey.   106
76. Magical M.A.N.T.R.A.: I meet cynicism and divisiveness with love.   107
77. Magical M.A.N.T.R.A.: I declutter what no longer serves me.   108
78. Magical M.A.N.T.R.A.: I am the keeper of the light.   109
79. Magical M.A.N.T.R.A.: I have faith in life as it unfolds before me.   110
80. Magical M.A.N.T.R.A.: I am in the business of relationships.   112
81. Magical M.A.N.T.R.A.: I am fine, one day at a time.   113
82. Magical M.A.N.T.R.A.: I am grateful for awareness.   114

TO MY BUTTERFLIES   115

83. Magical M.A.N.T.R.A.: I believed I could, so I did.   116
84. Magical M.A.N.T.R.A.: I have an abundance of faith.   117
85. Magical M.A.N.T.R.A.: I live a virtuous life.   118
86. Magical M.A.N.T.R.A.: I know humanity is my race and love is my religion.   119
87. Magical M.A.N.T.R.A.: I am going to shine my light so bright.   120
88. Magical M.A.N.T.R.A.: I choose me, now I'm free.   121
89. Magical M.A.N.T.R.A.: I am spiritually awake.   122

90. Magical M.A.N.T.R.A.: I am becoming perfectly. — 123
91. Magical M.A.N.T.R.A.: I let go into the effortless flow. — 124
92. Magical M.A.N.T.R.A.: I matter and can change the world for the better. — 125
93. Magical M.A.N.T.R.A.: I am bolstered by amazing and inspiring stories. — 126
94. Magical M.A.N.T.R.A.: I have a magical imagination. — 127
95. Magical M.A.N.T.R.A.: I know that sometimes the best ideas come heaven sent. — 128
96. Magical M.A.N.T.R.A.: I connect to my colorful soul. — 129
97. Magical M.A.N.T.R.A.: I dream big and default to a miraculous mindset. — 130
98. Magical M.A.N.T.R.A.: I don't forget to get my Vitamin SEA. — 131
99. Magical M.A.N.T.R.A.: I choose the greatest of all virtues – love. — 132

TO MY BUTTERFLIES — 133
GET READY: WHAT ARE YOU WAITING FOR? — 135

SECTION IV. TIME TO SPARKLE AND SHINE — 137

100. Magical M.A.N.T.R.A.: I set my own pace to gain clarity. — 138
101. Magical M.A.N.T.R.A.: Keep going - beautiful ones, we got this. — 140
102. Magical M.A.N.T.R.A.: I shine my light and enjoy what the universe offers. — 141

TO MY BUTTERFLIES — 143

103. Magical M.A.N.T.R.A.: Be impeccable with what follows the great I AM. — 144
104. Magical M.A.N.T.R.A.: Instead of going negative, I get curious. — 145
105. Magical M.A.N.T.R.A.: I choose to spread love. — 146
106. Magical M.A.N.T.R.A.: I get to choose. — 148

107. Magical M.A.N.T.R.A.: I choose love over fear and all the obstacles disappear. — 149
108. Magical M.A.N.T.R.A.: I get ready to be ready. — 150
TO MY BUTTERFLIES-THE FINALE — 151
Epilogue — 152
Acknowledgments — 155
About The Author — 159

Also by Meg Nocero — 163

PRAISE FOR SPARKLE & SHINE

"Sparkle, Sparkle, Sparkle! Whenever I think of Meg, I think of only positivity and magic. Ever since meeting her, she has inspired me every day. She teaches me that if you can be anything, be kind and that everything will get better. It does not matter what it is, you will shine through. 'Just when the caterpillar thought her life was over, she learned to fly.' Meg's positivity reaches you from over a thousand miles away. I don't know what I'd do without her. She radiates nothing but good energy and love in everything she does. *Sparkle and Shine* is no exception. This book is full of amazing vibes and I think everyone can use a little Meg to brighten their day."

~*Lily Shea Woods*, Youth Leader

"You have feet touched down in the here and now as well as the spirit world beyond. It is why things can be so difficult. You can see what others do not. You always have. It's awesome that you have found the words to share these experiences with the rest of us. You are so talented and brave. Can't wait to see the path you clear and the stardust that follows."

~*Dr. Alicia Eliscu*, DVM, Veterinary Surgeon

"Meg has been my best friend for 30 years. As my friend, she has been there to help guide me through some of the lowest points in my life. She has an amazing way of combining gentle compassion with the can-do motivation of a good coach. Her true gift is helping people see that they matter and that they have a right to the metaphorical 'seat at the table.' What comes through in her writing is her authentic experiences. She is exactly what you read, see or hear. There is unwavering courageousness in Meg to always be who she is, whether it's amazing or embarrassing. She puts it all out there. All of her inspiration, desire to motivate and drive to help bring relatableness to her writing. I am so happy so many people, besides her close friends, get to benefit from her love and support through her books!"

~*Lisa Lommerin*, E.S.L. Teacher, Wellness Coach

"Meg speaks magic into my soul! Her insight and positivity always give me the motivational push I need to keep moving forward. As an empath, I always need to be aware of the words I am repeating in my head. It is so easy to get consumed by the noise of the world around and take in negativity. Meg's words always make me connect back to the love within me and allow me to re-focus on my goals. Her book is like having a magical friend by my side with the perfect words to uplift my soul."

~*Jessica Quesada*, a.k.a. Ms. Brightside, Community Service Leader

"*I am enthusiastic about life* is Magical M.A.N.T.R.A. #5, which perfectly describes Meg! Yes, Meg is the real deal and she truly lives the wisdom that she shares. She has a wholehearted commitment to living her best life with so much joy and passion that it is contagious! Her first book, *The Magical Guide to Bliss* is a permanent fixture on my nightstand, and I look forward to its wisdom each night before bed. Now, with *Sparkle and Shine*, she has offered me a beautiful way to start my day by *choosing* how I want to move out into the world. Yes, Meg reminds us that we get to choose, and the reader will feel her cheering them on, every step of the way. I am grateful for Meg and for her wide-open heart. Our world needs more women like her!"

~*Tanya Mikaela*, Author of *The Circle, A Woman's Guide to Joy, Passion and Authenticity*

"*Sparkle and Shine* is pure magic, positivity, and passion. Passion to live life to the fullest, the joy to see life and all that it brings in a positive way, and the magical touch of every word on my soul. This book is warmth, love, and a guide to living life like the adventure it was meant to be. These M.A.N.T.R.A.s will get you moving forward when you are stuck, pausing when you need to breathe and kicking butt when you need to push through and be the SHEro of your story. Meg has captured magical tidbits in this easy to read volume. Love your Magical Unicorn."

~*Francisca Phillips*, Engagement, D & I Manager, Royal Caribbean Cruises, Ltd.

"*I accept myself wholly and completely*, this first M.A.N.T.R.A. reminded me of Renee Zellweger's famous quote from the movie *Jerry Maguire* when she said, 'you had me at hello.' This first affirmation is Meg at her authentic best. She has definitely done it again. By clearly expressing what she knows to be true and has had to learn the hard way, she waved her magic wand to produce these truly life transformational affirmations. I know too well that the body hears what the mind says and we truly are what we think! Kudos to Meg for shining her light and love into these magical M.A.N.T.R.A.s everyone should be saying and possibly yelling from the rooftops. I have no doubt this will be a bestseller!"

~*Maria Vina-Rodriguez*. Trusted Real Estate Advisor

"Meg once again harnesses her experiences, creativity and positivity, this time to successfully introduce folks to the simplicity, power and expansiveness of the spoken word - merging mantras and affirmations in a way that invites all of us to grow in and through love, resilience and self-awareness. The light she brings through her writing is energizing, empowering and impactful, which is much appreciated and so needed these days."
~*Rico Sogocio*, Reiki Master, Federal Judge

"Inspiring words all around from Meg. I feel a new sense of purpose and wonder from the words on the page, and they have truly inspired me in my day to day life. If you're looking for inspiration, look no further. Another great piece of work from a great author."
~*Patrick Scanlon*, Communications Major, Villanova University, Class of 2024

"The words, *Brighten Your Day and Lighten Your Way*, are the perfect description for Meg's M.A.N.T.R.A.s. Meg's words are always filled with positivity, enlightenment and impact. Whenever I interact with her, whether in person or through her publications, somehow she manages to extract the good from every situation. She has been blessed with this gift and I am so excited that she is sharing it with the world. During a time where most people complain, it's so refreshing to hear such an encouraging voice. Meg, continue to let your light shine so others' eyes can be opened to the good that is around them."
~*Dr. Delene P. Musielak* - Physician, Best Selling Author, Speaker, Coach, Entrepreneur

"M is for Meg, the newest addition to my periodic table of MUST HAVES. I liken this author and friend to that of an oxygen tank.

She offers life sustaining support which elevates and moves you. Science has long found that positive emotions are the root of human motivation - *Sparkle & Shine* feeds your spirit, settles into your subconscious and soul. The power of the words on these pages will uplift, inspire and reinvigorate your being. Readers are encouraged to read often."

~*Ieshia Haynie*, Executive Director, The Optimist Club of Overtown

"Another magical masterpiece by Meg Nocero! *Sparkle & Shine: 108 Mantras to Brighten Your Day and Lighten Your Way* inspires me to be my BEST me! My favorite mantra: #52, *Today I step forward into the effortless flow of life!* I am open to everyone who crosses my path and every new experience I encounter - for whatever shows up holds purpose on my journey! There are no mistakes; everyone and everything happens to us for a reason!"

~*Miranda Wilson*, E.L.A. Teacher & Wellness Coach

"Meg's book magically brings the best out of everyone. By refusing to accept anything less than what is ideal, she incorporates daily mantras to encourage you to stay the course that is true to yourself and aligns with your purpose. She will change your direction and reenergize you along the way. You will want *Sparkle and Shine* as your handbook in any transformative process. I am so grateful Meg has shared this work especially during these difficult times."

~*Randee Lehrer* RN, MBA, ACC, Founder & CEO of Energrowth Coaching LLC

"I am honored to be a member of the *Perfect "10" Club*. Meg has set the standard for what it means to be a strong, passionate and endlessly capable woman. Her words and stories provide direction, support, and inspiration when we need it most. While much of the world 'numbs out' when life is hard, that is not the divine path for any of us. Meg's words are metaphorical hands that hold ours while we walk the tough paths. No metamorphosis is easy in nature, and metamorphosis is not easy spiritually, physically, or emotionally for any of us. But hard doesn't matter. What matters is why we choose our paths and that with love, we have already 'arrived' well before any destination."

~*Sommer Sherrod*, Vice President, Healthcare Strategist

DEDICATION

The Perfect "10" Club Motto

1. I accept myself wholly and completely
2. My life is full of wondrous things, I just need to open my eyes & look
3. I make the world a better place & bring a random act of kindness in everything I do
4. Thank God for all my miracles today
5. Everything Happens for a Reason
6. I am Happy and Healthy
7. I am Loved and Beautiful
8. I am Strong and Smart
9. I am Successful and Grateful
10. I am Blessed!

Dedicated to all of those perfectly flawed members of the *Perfect "10" Club*. All of you who get up, despite your perceived flaws and imperfections and continue to do your best to make a difference in this beautiful world - your love affirms for me all that is wonderful and good.

Special dedication to my soul sister Janet Woods, my sisters Mary and Aimee and to my animal guides, my Shetland Sheepdogs, Leonardo Alfredo, and Luciana Josefina.

FOREWORD

"Good. Better. Best. I shall never let it rest. Til my good is my better and my better is my best!" ~unknown

I remember having to recite the above every day as a 3rd grader in Mrs. Cargile's class at Washington Elementary School. I grew up in Gary, Indiana and little did I know that the above mantra was going to be something that would help me throughout my whole life when I felt like throwing in the towel.

Like that mantra helped me, this book of mantras/affirmations/confessions will propel you to a better *you!* There's something about speaking out loud and letting words get in to your inner most being. There's something about doing it repetitively. There is something about making a conscious decision to do this, speak positive affirmations, every day that can lead to a life of greater fulfillment. I am always surprised at how this practice can

FOREWORD

be used for both the good and the bad. Have you ever noticed that if you get up, look outside and see that it's raining saying out loud (mantra/affirmation/confession) that it's going to be a bad day, a bad day is usually on its way?! How about when you say out loud that you are ready to dance in the rain, the rain usually becomes a musical symphony? Those things you tell yourself impact your perspective. Words are so powerful.

Meg Nocero has done it again with this book of 108 M.A.N.T.R.A.s! Filled with positive affirmations for different areas of your life, if you read it daily it is sure to bring results that are lasting! I'm always amazed by Meg! Her *can-do* demeanor and superb outlook on life is contagious! As you read these mantras and say them every day, you too will transform from the inside out and see radical change in your life.

Remember, your one mantra away from living your best life!

Dr. Jessica L. Mosley

Servant-Leader of *MizCEO*, Sovereign Care Medical Training Center, and Deborah's Place for Battered Women
    www.mizceo.com
    www.sovereigncaremtc.com
    www.deborahsplace.net

PROLOGUE

*D*on't Forget that to Sparkle & Shine, Schedule Time to Chase Butterflies!

"Real change, enduring change happens one step at a time." **Ruth Bader Ginsberg, Associate Justice of the Supreme Court of the United States, 1933-2020.**

---

*N*avigating this world seems to be a bit overwhelming these days.

It seems like this is a moment in history where emotions from the right and the left are running at an all-time high. Feeling called to do something to make this a world a better place, I know that it is non-action that will one day fill each of us with regret if we don't try.

Inspiration comes from many places. I am reminded to be present and aware even when my mind races. Knowing full well that we will all at one point be held to stand the trial of time, I can't let expectations unfulfilled stop me without reason or rhyme.

As I make decisions as to which direction to climb, I engage a mindful practice to embrace those choices of mine. And yes, now more than ever, schedule some time, to chase those butterflies to bring to life a beautiful vision and paradigm. And, I know this is one of the ways that we all can sparkle & shine.

For my friends, look up to the sky, there they are, those butterflies. And truth be told, they need no permission to fly so high. They have no limits, so why should I? So let yourself go, the time is nigh. Embrace your own mantra, use your imagination, surrender to love and close your eyes.

See clearly that each life that surrounds you is a part of the collective consciousness, the whole, and is ready to shine. Elevate your spirit and hope, allow your imagination and insights to get into line. Mantra after mantra, new energy infiltrates as you transform and get ready to magnify. Chase happiness and embrace joy - take off - your sparkly wings are strong, it is time to fly!

INTRODUCTION

What is a mantra?

    The Merriam-Webster dictionary defines a *mantra* as a sound, word, or phrase that is repeated by someone who is praying or meditating expressing a basic belief. The origin and etymology of *mantra* comes from Sanskrit, sacred counsel, formula, from *manyate* he thinks; akin to Latin *mens* mind. A mantra can be used like an affirmation to catapult your life in an incredibly positive direction. By repeating one out loud or internally that resonates with you, you are recalibrating the neural pathways in your brain to habituate around something that can be incredibly powerful. A mantra practice can be one of your tools that brightens your day and lightens your way if you incorporate it with consistency into your daily living. I know that it is safe to say, we need positive, uplifting habits now more than ever.

What is magical?

    The Merriam-Webster dictionary defines magical as an extraordinary power or influence seemingly from a supernatural source. The origin and etymology of *magical* comes from Middle English *magique*, from Latin *magice*, from Greek *magikē*, feminine of *magikos* Magian, magical, from *magos* magus. When we adhere to that which is magical, mystical, or spiritual in our lives, something inside of us changes on a deep and profound level. Our souls wake up, our minds are enlightened, and our hearts are capable of experiencing love from a place of incredible stirring beauty. Like the Three "Magi" (Wise ones) mentioned in the Gospel of Matthew in the Bible, we can tap into the magic that pulls us forward to follow our proverbial North Star that could lead to something or someone amazing. For many, seeing the world through magical eyes can lead to a life full of miracles. And to quote one of the greatest magical minds, Roald Dahl, British novelist and author of *Charlie and the Chocolate Factory*, "And above all, watch with glittering eyes the whole world around you because the greatest secrets are always hidden in the most unlikely places. Those who don't believe in the magic will never find it." When we start to ask and believe, we can see a different world before us getting ready to receive all that is has to offer.

What is a Magical M.A.N.T.R.A.?

A magical mantra can be just the thing that shifts and uplifts your life to experience more joy and bliss. Think about the word mantra as an acronym: M.A.N.T.R.A. For the purpose of this book, it stands for Magical Affirmations Now Transform our Reality into an Adventure. When we embrace a daily practice of magical affirmations, we can reinforce positive thinking now so that our experience on this life journey can become something that engages all of our senses at higher vibrations. From that magical place, there is no telling what wonderful things can happen. When we raise our positive vibes today by engaging a simple practice that turns into a positive habit, our lives can be

INTRODUCTION

embraced as an amazing adventure. Like a caterpillar surrenders to its journey of change into the darkness of the cocoon, with a magical mantra practice, at the end of the cycle, we can all emerge renewed into a spiritual freedom that marks a new beginning embracing our own beauty reaching new heights, just like the butterfly.

HOW TO USE THIS BOOK

This book sets out to inspire the reader to embrace their magic within through the practice of M.A.N.T.R.A.s, or reinforced positive affirmations and thinking. This book offers a supplement to the wisdom in my guide, the award-winning *The Magical Guide to Bliss, Daily Key to Unlock Your Dreams, Spirit & Inner Bliss*; it is a handbook that keeps the reader moving forward on their hero's journey with daily tools to help with their amazing transformation.

This book is divided into three main parts (Ask, Believe and Receive) and a final section (Get Ready-What are You Waiting For?) Each part has a section (inspired by Mary Oliver's poem, *Instructions for Living a Life*: Pay Attention, Be Astonished, Tell All About It) made up of 33 M.A.N.T.R.A.s. Notably, the significance of the number 33 is meant to embody this master teacher's number with deep spiritual and religious meaning. The last section (Time to Sparkle & Shine) sets out 9 M.A.N.T.R.A.s that prepare the reader to get ready to take a leap of faith to fully sparkle & shine.

There are 108 M.A.N.T.R.A.s in total that will help you to adopt, guide or start your own magical affirmation practice. In eastern philosophy, the significance of the number 108 is considered to be a sacred number of wholeness of existence - when you come to the end of the circle, like a string of Hindu prayer beads called *malas*, can also look to rosary beads in Christianity, you complete the M.A.N.T.R.A.s and catapult to another level of peace.

Like the insights in my first book *The Magical Guide to Bliss*, the M.A.N.T.R.A.s in *Sparkle & Shine* are written in a modular format. You choose how you would like to read it. If you prefer, you can read it straight through from beginning to the end. However, you can read the entries in any order. I chose this modular format to provide a condensed, easily accessible format for the busiest person. As a bonus, there are 11 inspirational letters in text boxes throughout from me to you.

The Content pages present a list of the M.A.N.T.R.A.s in each part and section as a reference to look through to address what affirmation you may be seeking on a particular day. Or, you can just set an intention and open up this book and let synchronicity pave the way. You just might pick the perfect M.A.N.T.R.A to brighten your day and lighten your way.

So, let's continue the journey with this *Sparkle & Shine* handbook and develop a new uplifting affirmation practice, one M.A.N.T.R.A. at a time. We got this!

Ask

SECTION I. PAY ATTENTION

"Assume the feeling of the wish fulfilled and observe the route that your attention follows." Neville Goddard, American author of *The Power of Awareness*, 1905-1972.

1. Magical M.A.N.T.R.A.: *I ask to be a charming gardener who plants seeds of love.*

    I stand from a place of love. There is pain and I feel it. There is hurt and I want to help heal it. There are those who divide and I reach out my hand to anyone who needs to take it. I do my part, where I can to teach ways to love more. To see different colors, genders and otherwise, I get to know the beauty from our differences and unite from a desire to peacefully coexist. I see so many souls collectively interacting on this journey. Meeting each one from a place of love sends a ripple effect that is palpable. Hate is extinguished and open wounds begin to heal. Now more than ever I need to be a charming gardener who plants beautiful seeds of love. I ask to see the beauty on a rainy day. I ask that an abundance of love drives the hate away. I choose to lift others up so we rise together instead of fall. I ask to bring the light of love for it conquers hate after all.

2. Magical M.A.N.T.R.A.: *I am decisive as I speak my dreams into existence.*

Don't let a lengthy discussion of "What Ifs" get in your way. You can wake up and empower yourself each and every day. Nothing is certain, so set your intentions well and dream big. Decide that progress incrementally moving you forward is a wonderful way to live. Speak confidently and set out your dreams, the universe's creative genius is just a whisper away. Know that if you don't ask, you lose a chance of what could be today. Are you willing to let fear stop you from choosing a path to set your dreams free? If the answer is no, time to set your goals and decide what you want to see. Magic unfolds when you take a leap; it is an exhilarating experience that you get. Get decisive with your life, speak your dreams into existence and you will most likely have no regret.

3. Magical M.A.N.T.R.A.: *I am worthy of love.*

I am worthy of love, it is my birthright. This is what I am repeating today. Now let me begin to say. First, I must choose to love myself. Second, I step away from co-dependency. Third, I must really start to embrace fully my lovely "corps & esprit" (body & spirit.) I remember this today as I navigate the waters of my inner storm. I will replace judgment with kindness for love to truly take form. I ask to focus on my soul as I breathe life into me. I know that a healthy respect for my journey will protect me from the disease to please. I am less likely to give away my power when I show up with authenticity. I place thoughts in my mind that welcome love and I start to pay attention to what I see. I am worthy of love, and welcome a life living with an open heart. To seek to understand then be understood, is clearly a worthy start.

To my Butterflies:

If you find yourself in spiritual darkness, please hold onto your beautiful light. Your light is what will keep you on the path of enlightenment to continue this worthy fight. You matter - right now - in this moment. Please hold on, be steadfast and true – if you turn on your light, together we will stand strong - that is me and you.

Do you believe in synchronicity? You know, those incidents of spiritual significance that ask us to consider the possibility of the divine. Experiences that seem serendipitous that engage our attention to the seemingly sublime. I do and was wondering if this may be just one of those times. As you read this letter asking you to beam brightly from a place of bliss and just shine.

The world needs a chance to liberate from darkness my beautiful friend. Your gifts are needed to show up with enthusiasm so that suffering can end. So much pain, Mother Earth is calling for an outpouring of love and kindness if we decide. It takes great faith and determination, but together we will reach that goal so that all of us can enjoy the ride.

I Love You,

Meg

4. Magical M.A.N.T.R.A.: If I stay focused, everything will be just fine.

Moment to Moment. Engage, enjoy, embrace each present moment. Be all there, be all in. Look the other in the eye. Live, laugh, love. Be ready to forgive. The here and now demands your full focus. Moment to moment. Look back and reminisce over each past moment. Remember from whence you came, each experience that has made you who you are today. Cherish each precious gift. Moment to Moment. Visualize, dream big, and act as if it all will come true in each future moment. Get enthusiastic and excited for what is to come. Be grateful for the unfolding of everything under the sun. Moment to Moment. If you stay focused, everything will be just fine. Do your best, nothing labeled bad or good is permanent over time. Moment to moment. Be proud of your life - no regrets, perhaps this affirmation is a sign.

5. Magical M.A.N.T.R.A.: *I am enthusiastic about life.*

Enthusiasm is contagious. Even when you look at the meaning of the word *enthusiasm*, one can experience an intense and eager enjoyment as defined in the dictionary. The etymology or derivation of the word *enthusiasm* can be traced to the Greek root *entheos* which means "in God"- inhabited and guided by the life force itself. What a word and feeling to spread around. When one gives in to it, enthusiasm wraps around you with excitement that bubbles over on to others. Start to engage your life from a place of enthusiasm and no doubt more positives will show up. Apply enthusiasm to your purpose and you will tackle any challenge with definite resolve. The enthusiastic ones always bring joy back to life. When I am enthusiastic, I come alive again with passion that bursts from within. Shake things up with enthusiasm and it will literally spice up your life.

6. *Magical M.A.N.T.R.A.: Stay present, no day but today.*

The morning sun greets you and welcomes a new day. You ask only this. When you make your daily wish, stay present. Time passes, to be still is a challenge to behold. What story is written, what experiences unfold. Look for things to celebrate. Bask in the becoming, blossoming, and beautifying. Distractions no more. Living out your dreams, no time to live from a place of fear. In this present moment, you don't have to imagine - this is your reality right here. No better day to start anew. There is no other path, just start walking through. Pay attention or you'll miss it. This is all created for you. No day like today.

7. Magical M.A.N.T.R.A.: I am enough, today I seek ways to tap into my source.

I am enough. I say it out loud. I hold a picture in my mind of all my achievements as a result of showing up each day. I am so proud. As the vast beauty of heavenly bodies float effortlessly around the sun, the universe does not need my permission to do its thing. We are one. Each one of us is a part of this miraculous and beautiful world, we get to choose how to tap into our source. Although we are all just small specks in the grand show, we still can be a mighty force. I am enough where I stand - let that positive energy expand. Through meditation, visualization and gratitude, I align with the universe and shift my attitude. For when I declare I am enough, it is time for me to see. I am here to manifest in this life the most amazing me.

8. *Magical M.A.N.T.R.A.: I am happy, magical and magnificent me.*

"Watch your thoughts, they become your words; watch your words, they become your actions; watch your actions, they become your habits; watch your habits, they become your character; watch your character, it becomes your destiny."
Lao Tzu, the founder of Taoism and the author of *Tao Te Ching*.

Seeing possibilities and embracing today, I declare I am happy. I am ready for positive change. Worrying robs me of the gift of the present and all of its gains. I declare I am magnificent me, my words catapult action to guide me through the rain. The mere fact that I am a creation of the divine is a sweet refrain. I stand in this truth as that is all that remains. Each habit is ingrained in character, I am here for great purpose and that I entertain. Boldness and unfettered optimism and a chance to walk down memory lane. Positive attributes flood my senses, for that I'll never complain. Not knowing what the future holds, I am happy to discover it again and again. Nothing is set in stone. Yet, my hope is renewed – that I will proclaim. If I let it, I will always have a chance to reawaken my happy heart unchained.

9. Magical M.A.N.T.R.A.: I am at peace, then balance will follow.

If it is balance I seek, I must intend to be at peace. To find a place of stillness and calm, I am encouraged to engage the child within. I play in my surroundings creatively looking to find colors that soothe my mind. Splashes of yellow bring on happiness. Shades of indigo and purple heal. And, soft blue brings a sense of calm to the fears. Then, I allow gentle music to caress my ears. If I set out 21 days to make this a healthy habit, just 10 minutes of peace a day can offer more stability throughout the year. Let's see how this goes with balance as my worthy goal. If my center is calm, I will feel better with more equilibrium from head to toe. Slowing down my breath and focusing on comforting colors to behold, I slowly become an instrument of peace- let that truth be told.

10. Magical M.A.N.T.R.A.: *I am a co-creator with the universe.*

That's right, I am looking to create and I know I don't have to go it alone. I ask that collaborators appear, with big ideas that match my own. There are many of you out there just waiting to take flight. Not for fame or fortune, just for pure delight. My intention has always been about following the dream. I know to go far, I really would prefer to get there together and pick up more steam. Whether I co-create with an artist whose one desire is to bring more color to a gray world or a writer who yearns to leave a better story for humanity; or a lawyer who uses her craft for justice or a doctor who digs deep to find enlightenment for a cure. I feel the tremendous tug at my creative strings. When I work with others, the universe allows us all to start to sing. Explode with the beauty of your calling and join me on this magical ride. Why not? It's more fun with others by your side.

1. Magical M.A.N.T.R.A.: I believe in my unlimited potential.

Are you ready to make a huge shift? Well, today is the day. Yes, it's true. Repeat after me, you are unlimited potential and no one can take that truth from you. Here is the missing link that will get you unstuck, introducing the unequivocal belief in your incredible luck. This moment holds a great opportunity to wake you up from your sleep. Grab the promise of a beautiful life that is waiting for you to keep. To recognize that you are made of God-stuff, good stuff, a spirit whose potential shines through. There is no better time than the present to gift this knowing to you. Create a life that suits you and your talent will pull you through. If negativity has reared its ugly head and threatens to overwhelm you. HALT, re-examine your "why" and then continue to just do what you do. Belief is so powerful, with a determined faith something wonderful is about to happen. Believe in your unlimited potential and the universe will conspire in your favor. What are waiting for? Stop slackin.

12. Magical M.A.N.T.R.A.: *I will make the day better for another.*

I will make the day better for another. This statement will not fall on deaf ears. Why? Because it is the kind of statement that embodies joy, kindness and care. Generosity of spirit can actually save you - about this did you know? When you are busy beating yourself up, here is a place you can go. Focus on helping another and you will be amazed at what it can do. You get to actually offer love to a family member, friend, colleague or even a stranger too. From a place of service, the result of your actions can literally change you. By shifting focus off of yourself, your problems and your sadness, you can reach out to another and do something to bolster gladness. Then, asking how you can make another's day better, this might just be the shift needed to transform. If you need a suggestion, sit down and write a gratitude letter that's warm. Give service to the beautiful souls on Earth to help their dreams come true, bolsters your soul to awareness and allows your SHINE to come on through.

To my Butterflies:

Now is as good a time as any to wake up and begin anew. Time to clarify how you want to live. Look around - you are surrounded by diverse people whose gifts and talents are the seeds that will ensure a peace-filled future for all of us. As long as that is your focus, then the future will remain bright. As long as you find your voice amidst the noise, you will be alright. Celebrate today, from this point on, let go to peace and it turns into another kind of fight.

A fight for love, you won't allow the sacrifices to be forgotten through the anger and tears. Be clear about this though, there is great power and opportunity with "We the People" as you sign up to form a more perfect union. All people must be represented at the table. You and I are the unfolding of the intentions of our forefathers, it is our journey. This letter asks for you to level up, embrace equality; we cannot go silently into the night. We must empower each other to use our voices and talents towards a new day. We must empower each other to wake up for there is much work to be done. Ready to move forward, we transform into something even better along the way. And we hold each other accountable. Wake up my friends, do your part - for tomorrow we march - it is a new day.

I Love You,

Meg

13. Magical M.A.N.T.R.A.: *All is well.*

Repeat after me, "All is Well." Take a deep breath, "All is Well." Hold your hand over your heart, feel it beating - "All is Well." Start the minute you wake up to reset and recalibrate from this place. Pay attention to the way you feel each time you state, "All is Well." If you want to put the brakes on the craziness before it gains momentum and overwhelms you- just sit, stop, and say it again and again - "All is Well." Now close your eyes and imagine your resistance dissipating as you elevate to a higher feel good plane. The minute you open your eyes think about one thing that makes you excited to face the day again. All is Well.

14. Magical M.A.N.T.R.A.: I am a divine masterpiece.

I am a divine masterpiece. A work of amazing artistry. From the top of my crown to the soles of my feet, every inch of my body works together, I am complete. Acceptance with gratitude for the color of my hair. I look in my eyes and with wonder - I stare. My skin is divine, my nose sits just right. My head held so proud, my jaw a sculpted delight. Whenever I feel shame or a bit uncomfortable too, I shut down the negative self-talk because I know what I have to do. I am perfectly unique, there is no model made the same. And, I wear my tiara, I am proud of my name. I am human - a miracle. I am in awe of synchronicity that brought me to this world. God, the creator, and my parents did well, I giggle with delight and twirl. I am a divine masterpiece. There you go, I said it again. And when you forget you are too, I will be sure to remind you as well my friend.

15. Magical M.A.N.T.R.A.: *I give myself my own approval.*

People are literally dying to get noticed. Their one goal is to post something that goes viral. They pretend to be someone they are not and do stupid things just to get attention. Social media is all about who is seen and how many likes. It is a place that displays a fake reality, portraying a very perfect picture life. People who seek approval from others will do anything to be in the limelight. This kind of behavior can ultimately steal your sanity. One day you are on top of the world, the next everything falls apart into a calamity. It's time to hold integrity close at hand - it's time to stand up for your own worth. Take your power back, shine your own light - through your own inner beauty inherit the earth. The disease to please keeps you trapped, you give in to your own removal. That is until you decide, I give myself my own approval.

16. Magical M.A.N.T.R.A.: *I don't have to figure it all out, just focus on love.*

Today I give myself permission to feel whatever feelings come: from joy to gratitude - from sadness to anger. I trust that this too shall pass and life unfolds exactly as it should. And as I connect the dots, I see the hand of the divine in everything. In all that I have accomplished so far and all the challenges too. I know I am not alone. I'm still learning day by day - I don't have to figure it all out. I just have to live my moments as they come. I focus on the good memories and am surrounded by the incredible love of family and friends. That love will always be my strength.

17. Magical M.A.N.T.R.A.: *I am authentically me.*

What is authentic? What is real or true? I laugh, I smile, I scream, I cry. This range of emotions is what makes me a genuine human whether I like it or not. Sometimes I am so in the moment, so centered that the effortlessness of life's beauty takes my breath away. Sometimes I am on a detour off the path and frustrated - feeling at times lost and unable to find my way back. Sometimes I am aligned to my calling and then sometimes I just don't know why I am here at all. I am not crazy - I am a beautifully intricate human being set loose on this journey to be as real as I can be given life's circumstances. And when I stand with this knowledge, I find peace at my core. I am authentically me showing up for what life has in store.

18. Magical M.A.N.T.R.A.: I am a great storyteller.

Live, laugh, love, repeat - over and over again. Let me tell you about a story of a girl who chose to dream big despite what she thought was her end. Life kept throwing punches, she didn't think she would survive. Instead of falling down, she decided to get up and thrive. Her laughter did return where she could choose to love with gratitude. It is amazing how life can change along with a fine-tuned positive attitude. She chose to tell a great story where she could inspire others to dream. Following the human arc of the hero gathering an amazing team. Life used to be so challenging, until she unwrapped her fears. She was way too determined to give up and now gets to enjoy her years. Live, laugh, love, repeat! What a wonderful beginning to the story. When you start from that place again are you ready to tell about your life's glory?

19. Magical M.A.N.T.R.A.: *I expect magic and miracles.*

Looking at my journey as an observer, I see life as a gift. Some would say I'm lucky, but I get what I expect - you get my drift. I am blessed with an amazing tribe by birth and by choice, this I know. I am blessed with amazing opportunities that showed me all the wonderful ways to go. And most of all, when I come to a crossroads facing change, I am blessed with a strong faith that I will make it resurrecting past the pain. I expect magic and miracles, I confidently surrender to this truth. Be still and know the force that surrounds me will carry me, there I will always find proof.

20. Magical M.A.N.T.R.A.: What God has for me, God has for me.

There is something deeply satisfying that comes with the knowing that the universe will conspire in your favor. There is an element of peace that arrives when you believe that your hard work inspired by an inner passion will deliver to you all that is good. There is something beautiful that overtakes you when you understand that this life is not about competition but co-creation. Because ultimately what God has for you, God has for you and no mere mortal can take that away.

21. Magical M.A.N.T.R.A.: I am dancing with the universe today.

"The greatest human activity occurs in regard to your relationships with not only loved ones but also the very cosmos and, ultimately, God." **Dr. Michael Anthony Nocero, Jr., my father.**

How I dance with life will sure to be my legacy. Today, I may prefer to rumba surrounded by beautiful friends. Tomorrow, salsa and cumbia alone with glee. I may take the lead today, then I shall follow you tomorrow. The dance of life will carry me always- one ballet step forward out of sorrow. Spinning with delight guided by my magical song; my body is free to move and nothing feels wrong. I engage the wonderful rhythm and move my feet along. I feel the beat of a drum whose drummer plays it strong. I am dancing with the universe today, I invite you on this incredible path. And if we stumble along the way, I promise you I won't laugh. Shall we dance magical ones before the day is through, we will always remember those moments that I will share with you.

2. Magical M.A.N.T.R.A.: Note to self, let sh*t go.

Yuck, yuck, yuck - tired of being stuck, stuck, stuck! One more day is too many - clearing out all the negative energy bind. Abundance awaits - declutter the mind. The more you release, the more you shall find. Purgatory no more - it's time to dance wonderfully on the floor. Nothing holding you back really my magical dears, just let go of those crazy, stupid fears. Release, reset, reawake - it is never ever too late. Dream big my shining ones, therein lies all sorts of fun. Let that sh*t go - with a greater faith - the rewards you will surely know. Having acquired the disease to please, you will prefer to stand tall and get up off your knees. You give too many people power over your life and your worth. As an adult, it is time to inherit the earth. Bring love, inspiration and kindness if you do, for that is what the world can offer you. No judgments, make your peace with the past, grateful for the beauty that remains. Transformation is not just for caterpillars and gets easier as you honor your domain. Light always shines when you tap into the great energy source and know, note to self, stay awake to your blessings and let that sh*t go.

23. Magical M.A.N.T.R.A.: I am a work in progress.

Pay attention and the mystery of life will gain more clarity. Today begins a 21-day positivity challenge, I dare thee. Do you accept? I guess it is about time. So, turn off the television and turn up some good music, you'll move just fine. Isn't that the beauty of life – to take a step back and give peace a chance? Who cares if you are flawed, as long as you engage the dance. With more positivity to attract, the brightest of lights is on you. Grateful for the people who show up optimistic through and through – with the best that is yet to come and it is only three weeks too. So, go out today with this positivity goal in mind - it's the collective consciousness anyway - energy overlap - if you could be so kind. You want peace - then leave perfection aside. Declare I am a work in progress, it's time to enjoy the ride.

24. Magical M.A.N.T.R.A.: I am discovering my beauty within.

Each person is a beautiful work of art. And, the inevitable changes that come with living, allow our beauty to evolve and grow into something even more amazing. Resilience or the capacity to quickly recover from challenges and strife, creates beauty from within that is seen throughout your life. Think about it - as an active participant on the journey, opportunities to improve show from here to eternity. A masterpiece and a work in progress too - the wisdom that comes with living is just so beautifully you. Just beautiful.

25. Magical M.A.N.T.R.A.: *I always believe that something wonderful is about to happen.*

Keeping my eyes on the prize, I declare to the world this way. May the universe bring me something wonderful and with it let me play. With the seriousness of life, I need to start out each day. Affirming a belief that good things lie ahead - for this, I pray. For all those who doubt, I have seen amazing things unfold. When I declare boldly and out loud, an incredibly story can be told. And when that something wonderful knocks on my door, there is no telling what magnificent things life has in store. And it will, so when it does be sure to let me know. This is a magical affirmation, remember you reap what you sow.

26. Magical M.A.N.T.R.A.: We've got this!

So, you think you lost your way somewhere along the road? Well, you're never really lost truly if truth be told. For sure, you travel this life with some challenges along the way. Sometimes you can handle it, while other times you feel dismay. Remember this when your light feels a bit dim, your true self remains calling to you from within. You were born with a purpose, this I know to be true. When you keep walking forward, you will find you walked right on through. Believe me, I have been there and I searched high and low, come alive again I begged to my wary soul. You just can't give up, unpack in the misery and the dark. For if you stay there, you will miss out on the spark. A spark of happiness or a glimpse of your shine, the beginnings of a smile that will return again over time. So, if you find yourself in that dark place not sure what to do, there are many who reach out and will be there for you. Incremental steps forward, side by side, you'll not be alone. When you make it out of the tunnel, love will carry you home. Be gentle with yourself. We've got this!

To my Butterflies:

Hold on to your dreams. Sometimes they may seem so big and impossible to realize that you just want to give up. But, remember it is the journey not the destination that is the whole point - the manifesting along the way. There are those things in life that infuse enthusiasm and passion into your days. There are those goals that give you the will and desire to wake up in the morning. And there is a little voice inside that says keep going, you are getting closer every day.

In the great big picture of life, your dreams are the things that give you the sustenance to go on. Especially during dark moments, you can hold on to your dreams for the energy to see you through. So whatever little or big dream you hold in your heart, know that will be the magic to help you create anew. Food for your soul. So, don't stop using your dreams and vision to catapult yourself forward. Remember the visionaries dreamt about flying to the moon before that dream came true. Who knows what wonderful things will happen next!

I Love You,

Meg

27. Magical M.A.N.T.R.A.: *I choose to live my life on my terms.*

You gaze right into those gorgeous eyes looking back at you in the mirror and see what your soul yearns for most. Hold your hands over your heart space and listen to it speak clearly. Bow your head to honor your choices as to how you will live your life. Now is the time to pay attention. You know what you need to do. Scream it out - cry it out - set out your terms and don't you dare give up on you. Life is too short to give away control to another to decide. No excuses you have only a once around - you will be proud of that as you hit your stride. Now go!

28. Magical M.A.N.T.R.A.: *Let's keep hope alive.*

Hope is at the center of your being. Hope to love better, to be loved. Hope to feel joy, to bring joy to another. Hope to awaken to purpose, to inspire others to do the same. You will never pass up an opportunity to pay hope forward, to inspire actions rather than blame. There is no better time than today to reset, refocus and renew hope for a better now and tomorrow. You will do your best to remember the fragility of life and the miracles that can happen when hope is introduced once again. It's quite a powerful elixir to alleviate pain and shine the light on possibility. Hope is the desire or expectation that something wonderful is about to happen when you believe. Please won't you help me and others to keep hope alive? Hold On, Pain Ends.

29. Magical M.A.N.T.R.A.: *I inspire magic.*

The world is ready to become a better place. We hear a cry for this from all creation. Many people are awakening, all sectors of humanity through awareness and inspiration. Our impact on nature and each other has shown, we all want better for this our collective home. Inspired to speak up so that a new consciousness takes over. This great pause that stopped everything has something wonderful about to spillover. These are magical times— inspire and let your dreams take flight. It is time to set out intentions, give up turmoil and the nasty fight. This beautiful new dawn where wonder and awe can be embraced. We choose to inspire magic, creative genius can't be replaced. A belief in all things possible - let that good news spread. We inspire magic daily, then time to rest and go to bed.

30. Magical M.A.N.T.R.A.: *I smile as a direct achievement.*

What greater goal in life is there then to bring joy to others? What greater accomplishment at the end of a day knowing you possibly helped to reduce another's pain? What better feeling to look around and see a beaming beautiful smile? What incredible delight to welcome someone drenched out of the rain? Picture it - share a smile that brings peace and understanding thereof. Delivered when most needed, a simple small gesture of love. You can collect material riches, but it's just not the same. Each amazing smile given, such happiness remains. If the foundation of my something wonderful is to share smiles just the same. I smile as a direct achievement and I will keep doing it again. Join me!

3 1. Magical M.A.N.T.R.A.: I choose an attitude of gratitude.

Attitude of gratitude - what are you grateful for? First thing in the morning and at the end of the day, make asking yourself this a habit and the blues fade away. A grateful heart and mind trained to be thankful for your blessings. Even for a vulnerable life with no window dressing. Looking for good as you go about your day, gratefulness is a habit that brings more goodness your way. Even for the uncertainty of life, give your appreciation. You can never be too grateful - as you move from station to station. Continuously you say it over and over again, for every step in your advancement and every person you call friend. When you shift your perspective to see life this way, life will continue to give you evidence, amazing things hoped for on the way.

32. Magical M.A.N.T.R.A.: *I obey my soul, from there I bloom with grace.*

Spiritually, grace is defined as a gift that involves love and mercy given to others even when we feel that they are less than perfect. It is an empowering word that comes from the Latin *gratia*, meaning pleasing or favor. It embodies the smooth elegance of forgiveness, letting go of past wrongs and an offering of a simple prayer or blessing. We imagine life calls for us to obey our souls and show up, regardless how imperfect we are. Embodying grace in all things, leaving seeds of love as we walk today. Wherever we are, there will always be an opening to welcome faith and gratefulness for the blessings of the bloom we will see one day. There still remains so much good in society. This is an invitation to celebrate those we know who through grace set us free from anxiety.

3. Magical M.A.N.T.R.A.: *There are no mistakes in my life.*

Live your life like there is no Plan B. Stick to your guns and let your vision unfold for you to see. Plan A all the way, nothing to require a back-up contingency too. Just set out a clear vision, then any road that you choose is perfect for you. Every opportunity you take is divinely inspired. There are no mistakes in life, no failures as long as you tried. The wisdom was necessary to tackle the next turn. Like a riddle to be solved, your acuity is sharpened as long as you learn. If you follow the ancient poet Rumi's advice, "Live life as if everything is rigged in your favor," you won't have to question twice. As you ask for your heart's desire, then it is all worth the labor. No regrets, no looking back and reap the rewards you will savor. Forward moving towards a distinct destination, every person who shows up you offer help with your chosen vocation. Unconcerned with the outcome, only looking for the magic. Even if you fall, to not get up would be tragic. There will be opportunities that come to grow and advance - stick to Plan A and give it a chance.

Believe

SECTION II. BE ASTONISHED

"There are only two ways to live your life. One is as though nothing is a miracle. The other is as though everything is a miracle." Albert Einstein, German physicist, 1879-1955.

34. Magical M.A.N.T.R.A.: *I originate from the extraordinary.*

What an amazing thought to get you started today. To channel the inner extraordinary, imagine standing in a brand-new pink superhero cape or rocking a shiny new crown. Revert to the child within and tap into the model of whichever superhero that inspired you then. Receive an illuminated vision, spreading love with purpose, infused with unwavering faith that all will unfold as it should. Pouring over with gratitude for this knowing, you are the miracle maker. With or without the cape, go out and do your thing, spread your extraordinary in the connections you meet. And remembering that you came from extraordinary, set out to do this without limits. See what superpowers emerge as magic and miracles come into existence.

35. Magical M.A.N.T.R.A.: *Loving myself fully is the best gift.*

Ever heard the word *namaste*? If you have ever taken yoga, at the end of the class the teacher will end with this word. It is a Sanskrit phrase that means, "the God in me bows to the God in you." Think about this. If God is in you, you are created in God's image, then truly loving yourself acknowledges your divinity too. If each living creature on this Earth is precious, then that means you must be too. So, look into the mirror at your reflection and soften your eyes from criticism or judgment, and repeat after me, "I love you." Each exchange, each hug, each kindness shown, will be returned to you. Each smile affirms a shared beauty. Each thank you embodies adoration. If hurt people, hurt people - then just imagine what loved people can do. The change begins with me and you.

36. Magical M.A.N.T.R.A.: *I am passionate about life and pursue my purpose.*

There is a magical enthusiasm that develops when you discover what you are passionate about. Excitement develops from this curious joy that arises when you finally stumble upon a path that resonates with your spirit. When you know what takes you closer to following a purpose-filled life, you will readily dismiss the blocks that get in your way. Once you match your passion to purpose, the inspiration will appear to see you through. Use this force to bring your dreams to life. Keep moving forward even through failure. When you repeat that "I am passionate about my life and pursue my purpose" without fail, the universe will help you out with all the details.

37. Magical M.A.N.T.R.A.: *I let my heart speak louder than my head.*

Visualize this today. Your heart is the center of love. Your blood is the joy that gets you going. As the steady beat of love pumps joy throughout, your body is nourished allowing your soul to thrive. This is the life force shared that keeps the magic of our existence alive. This is the joy that has you in awe of the reality you experience. This is the joy that gets you out of your monkey mind and into a peaceful state. Thoughts infused with feeling are powerful things. When you let your heart speak louder than your head, the joy that materializes can transform winter into spring. There what was broken and made you fear, becomes a beautiful song for all to hear.

To my Butterflies:

Reminder: let go or be dragged! To all of those who think letting go of past hurts or resentment is hard, I hear you. But you know what is harder? Holding on, letting the nastiness take residence rent-free in your head and wasting precious time focusing on what no longer serves you.

Seriously - whether it be feelings of unworthiness or thoughts that you are not enough, I want you to remember this one truth: you still have a choice. You get to choose where your attention goes. And butterflies, if you start to relax into the possibility that something better awaits, you will find it. If you let your mind release negativity so not to be dragged, you will start to fly. Release and be lifted effortlessly to greater heights. You really can make the shift as you get courageous to a higher calling, believing new gifts of love await you. No longer sabotaging your happiness when you do. Let go, pick yourself up, wipe yourself off, and move on.

I Love You,

Meg

38. Magical M.A.N.T.R.A.: *I run towards what I love.*

If you are feeling frustrated in life, then ask yourself one question: in this moment - are you doing what you love? If the answer is yes - then let your frustration go. But, if the answer is No, here are tips to help you grow. Set aside a day, an hour or a moment to just experience great joy. Do something life-infusing, play with a favorite toy. How you use your energy is a conscious choice. Perhaps now is the time to raise up your voice. You have talents. You have skills to do what you will. If you do what you love, then life becomes more amazing still. Say YES to your happiness and NO to your sorrow. Run towards the sun and chase your dreams for a brighter tomorrow. Run towards what you love and don't settle for less - PEACE will be the result of you doing what you do best.

39. Magical M.A.N.T.R.A.: *I move to the magical beat of the universe.*

I hear the soft chimes playing with the wind outside my window. Sounding off a delightful melody resting between gusts. The wind blows effortlessly against them as the music of life's dance is orchestrated. Enlivening all my senses, nature's symphony encourages me to embrace the day. My heartbeat aligns with the sounding of drums. It is the curtain call each day, just start playing along. Dance, sing, engage. The party has just begun. This dance called life needs to awaken with the rising sun. The dance allows for beauty in the transition of the human experience. I move to the magical beat of the universe that is so mysterious. It is a path to ultimate bliss!

40. Magical M.A.N.T.R.A.: *I ask, believe, and receive.*

I ask, believe and receive. It can be simple as that. Even the Bible teaches this lesson, in Matthew 7:7, read it stat. It says, "Ask, and it is given to you; seek, and you shall find; knock, and it will be open to you." If you start now, you won't waste your time. It is the ask after you set your intention, that will bring more sunshine. Definitely, it will get you ready to prime the pump. It is the belief that your wish is coming, stay in this space - don't jump. It is the receiving that welcomes your dream, your testimony will be given. But you have to know that all three lay out an equation for the driven. I ask you today embrace the role of believer. Only then will you see what the universe can deliver. After you ask the divine for what your soul needs, believe in all that is possible, and be open to receive. This magical trilogy won't lead you astray, I ask, believe and receive - what comes next leads to a brighter day.

4 *1. Magical M.A.N.T.R.A.: Expect what you want into your life.*

The "Accountability Bitch" Berta Medina reminds me all the time, "We hear a lot about manifestation and attraction, both important I assure you. However, I believe that in life, we may not always get what we want or even what we need, but we always get what we expect." So, with that in mind, start raising your expectations and all the universe will rise to greet you there. Just to be clear, I did not say raise your expectations of other people. This, my Butterflies, is all about You! How you show up on a daily basis. How you set out to match your intentions to opportunities. How you experience your life. The word expectation is defined as the strong belief that something will happen. This can go both ways. If you expect the worst, you will be looking for it. But, if you expect the best, then what will follow will most likely surprise you. And baby, I'll drink to that - coffee or champagne, your preference!

42. Magical M.A.N.T.R.A.: I remember I am a teacher and others are watching.

While actions speak louder than words, profound words coupled with inspirational actions can be the equation for incredible and positive change in a world desperate for it. Teach and act well so that those who look up to you can use your example to set the tone for an incredible life. There is always someone who will look to you for guidance, for wisdom, and for hope. Your life is the legacy you get to leave to the next generation and the next. A tradition of love! What story will you choose to leave behind? You are molding lives whether you like it or not - so choose impeccable words and be kind. As a teacher, I remember to be cognizant in what I do. As a student, I am ready to see what my teachers do.

43. Magical M.A.N.T.R.A.: Change is good, transformation even better.

Day transforms to night, night to day. The cycle of life continues bringing with it experiences that change us. Sometimes joyful, sometimes painful - but we are changed nonetheless. A process of maturation that none of us will escape, nor should we. Waking up to a new strength that we never knew – waking up once again to the beauty of a transformative life. One that has us really appreciating being alive, opening our hearts up to a world of good we would never have experienced before. Trust the process, don't quit– there are beautiful surprises that await. Like a butterfly born anew, transformation can be so great.

4. Magical M.A.N.T.R.A.: *I embrace my shine.*

Perhaps today is the perfect day to wear your tiara or crown and sparkle. Shine so bright that you leave a trail of glitter behind you. Be a good kind of selfish today and do the things that serve your highest good. A generous kind of self-love starts from the inside and emanates out. Lighting the way for others who follow you. This is your journey to bliss and there is no better time than now to make it as amazing as possible. Light up your life people – let's ride together and embrace our shine. Without effort, you do it all the time!

To my Butterflies:

To go through life numbing out is a worse fate. In August of 2001, I woke up in the middle of the night to a mysterious sound. It was a high-pitched ringing noise. In a fog, I pulled out the plug to the television that was located in my room, yet it did not go away. Looking for its origin without any luck, I sleepily retreated to the living room to find a refuge from this annoying sound that eerily reminded me of the sound of a tea kettle, ready to pop. No matter where I went it continued to follow me. And for months, feeling tortured, I let it immobilize me.

Years later, I see the gift in what I initially believed was a curse. Had I not gotten what is medically referred to as tinnitus, I still would be walking numb to life. But life, vita, breath, hope, and joy were all calling to me. I wanted to believe that I had a reason to be here. I had to accept and be fully present showing up authentically me. While I tried to numb out, I did not want to face the pain of loss because I did not know if I would survive it. This sound appeared and changed my life. I had to heal and allowed it to guide me.

In August of 2017, I resigned from a job that no longer aligned with my beliefs and purpose. My wakeup call led me on a path where I kept asking questions. I was getting curious as to what this beautiful life filled with beautiful people, animals, places and things had to offer me. And with the divine guidance, the path that led to consciousness helped me to keep my head above water and perhaps the ringing at bay. I was able to carve out a new existence fully aware in this present day.

There are days that the ringing is no longer there and other days it serves as a reminder to go within to find my center of calm. I believe it was my soul protesting. It wanted to love more, learn more and most definitely strive for better. Everyone has a breaking point, when the spiritual raging out says "that's enough!" I am grateful, to go through life numb for an exuberant spirit is too tough.

I Love You.

Meg

45. Magical M.A.N.T.R.A.: I create a plan to fulfill the greatest vision for my life.

Do you want to go on a magical adventure today? Before you take off, you must plan away. Get out your roadmap and get into sync. A fabulous journey is far easier than you think. Lots of wonderful things to see, lots of places to go. The happiest create a vision, only the daring will know. Want to live out the excitement of life and dreams to fulfill? Then clarify where you stand, there's no magical pill. No better plan of action, then to set out a plan. Study where you want to go. That first step is when the adventure began. The world is your oyster and the path you'll design. If you sit down and dream, possibility you'll find. So, do you want to go on a magical adventure this year? Grab your amazing plan and set out with no fear.

46. Magical M.A.N.T.R.A.: *I am pure perfection.*

What if everything happens for a purpose? What if everything happens for your highest good? What if the unfolding set out to teach you a lesson? Perhaps then the gift is in the learning, that is understood. What if you embrace the fact that what you are seeking is right there where you are? Today, stretch out your arms to the sky and just start reaching for the stars. Then wrap your arms around you - shoulder to shoulder in a butterfly pose. Just appreciate for one moment who you are, pure perfection – just like the petals and thorns of a rose.

47. Magical M.A.N.T.R.A.: I believe that the universe is unfolding exactly as it should.

Sometimes it has to be enough to believe in yourself. Just holding on to an unwavering faith and trust that everything will unfold as it should. There is no fast forward button for your own home movie. While you may wish to see the end - what would you do if you could? You can visualize a happy unfolding when you take an inventory of what you've done. Experiences and good memories, every day you wake up to see the rising sun. I start with a belief in myself- a positive attitude is so key. In hopes that something wonderful is about to happen, this idea gives me such glee. I believe that the universe is unfolding as it should, what's meant to be, will be.

48. Magical M.A.N.T.R.A.: *I believe that I have an obligation to shine.*

To shine in the midst of uncertainty is a quality held by the greatest visionaries of all time. With this positive attitude and belief in self, their ingenuity and innovation guide their rhyme. To witness the unfolding of greatness, it is a wonderful testament to inspiration. To motivate and encourage through example, is a blessing for any generation. Whether they are the forefathers and mothers who came before us, they all held true to a vision. Facing fears during any challenge, uniting the world is their mission. With an enthusiastic approach to life and belief that to shine is an obligation, all of us can be prepared to take on any transformation. Because that is what we are here for - to shine.

49. Magical M.A.N.T.R.A.: Forget about who you will follow, how will you lead?

Now is a perfect time in history to be the change that you wish to see. Instead of asking who shall I follow - a better question is "how shall I lead?" We need more leaders with integrity and respect for others, perhaps then we'll see. The moral compass that we wish to guide us into a better reality. Free to discover new awareness, empowered by love and mutuality. As leaders, we see problems, we look for solutions - a wholistic approach, not duality. There is a collective consciousness that we are a part of - no separation between you and me. At the grassroots level, we all need to become leaders of inspired action. We are just getting started - so ask yourself again, "how shall I lead?" and get some traction. It's not always easy to step up, but it's really necessary.

50. Magical M.A.N.T.R.A.: *I stand in my beauty and shine.*

You show the world how strong you are. Let hard work define you. Let perseverance guide you. You show the world how awesome you are. Let that message of wonderment ring true. Let that wonderful vision become you. You show the world how courageous you are. Let your authenticity guide the way. Let your unresolved anger dissipate and allow joy to take its place. You show the world how fabulous you are. Let grace bathe over you. Let your uniqueness as a child of love advance you confidently through. Stand in your beauty and shine!

5. 1. Magical M.A.N.T.R.A.: Success is in the heart of the beholder.

 Where beauty is in the eye of the beholder, a successful life resonates from the heart. Take a moment and get in touch with your song, this is a wonderful place to start. Does it play a joyful tune or one that weeps with sadness? Going within will stop the madness. It is at your heart's center, therein you'll meet your soul. To tune right in and go there, there is no better role. Are you looking to soar to great heights - fulfilled by all that it has to offer? Then take time for internal reflection, for this is what I have to proffer. At heart center you'll find your life's success, it is there that you will know. For the emotions of the heart speaks to your mind, it can take you so, so, high, or bring you down so low.

52. Magical M.A.N.T.R.A.: Today I step into the effortless flow of life.

No more fighting the current, it's time to go with it. The struggle is a creation of your ego. To truly experience true joy and the happiness that this day has to offer, you have to be open and willing to experience it as it comes. Every person who crosses your path, every experience that you encounter, even the timing of those events, all hold purpose on your journey. Guided by your divine intuition, no more begging, pleading or fighting. Honor your space and the space of others and just enjoy the flow. Whatever shows up offers wonderful guidance as long as you are open to it. And you might just enjoy yourself - imagine that!

53. Magical M.A.N.T.R.A.: *I fulfill my greatest potential.*

I fulfill my greatest potential. Say it out loud again. I fulfill my greatest potential. On this foundation, the most amazing life journey can unfold. Henry Ford, the founder of the assembly line technique and the Model T Ford, said, "Whether you think you can, or think you can't, you're right." In that vein, start with a belief that is so powerful that you can catapult forward to take the next best steps. Either an empowering or a limiting belief in your mind can have a direct impact on your body. To give you the best chance, choose your thoughts well. When you focus on your intentions and visualize the process that will get you there, it is a good beginning. It gets you ready to take the actions necessary to get you where you want to go. Thereby, I fulfill my greatest potential that started in the mind becomes the reality you will experience and want to know.

5 *4. Magical M.A.N.T.R.A.: I set out to enjoy the view.*

    So much beauty surrounds you, whatever you do. If your eyes look to the ground, how will you ever be able to enjoy the view? Seeking your value from wrong sources, leaves you disappointed and feeling blue. Questioning how you let others control your worth, how can that ever see you through? The journey is yours, these opportunities are gifts. Your life is a testament too. If you choose to see the world through others, you hand your power over – it's true. In order to follow your calling and do what you are here to do, you shift your perspective. And my friends, that's what you are going to do. You are here to make a difference, starting today you bid adieu. To everything that no longer serves you, look at the trail ahead, it sparkles and shines too. So grateful to those who remind you of the gifts awaiting for you. And, when you ask for guidance, you look up with grateful eyes and enjoy the view.

5. Magical M.A.N.T.R.A.: I am tethered to pure positive energy.

Believe in positive energy. That wonderful vibe that emanates from your soul. Bringing it along with positive inspiration, attracting goodness on the life path is a good role. Blessed with wonderful guidance throughout your life and your career. With gratitude for the journey, a myriad of beautiful faces do appear. Leaving their mark on your life forever, changed in so many wonderful ways. So happy to have all the wisdom, gives you hope for better days. You are tethered to pure positive energy. This is true even when you sink so low. Eventually, you bounce right back up again, the skies the limit and the place to go. To be mentored and to mentor, pay it forward is only right. You are tethered to the pure positive energy and with this can fight the good fight.

56. Magical M.A.N.T.R.A.: I create life's coming attractions in my imagination.

Albert Einstein said, "Imagination is everything. It is the preview of life's coming attractions." If you need a kick start to your imagination, buy a good book - it's a great transaction. One with an enticing title that helps you get out of your rut. A book can take you anywhere, it can even get you unstuck. Favorite books open your eyes to new perspectives. They open your heart to give your life wings. Books can open your world to new possibilities. A good story can show you interesting things. Whether it is a mystery or a romance, reading a book can take you away. To travel with the most fascinating people, see amazing new places or be exposed to interesting plays. Reading helps to boost your imagination's potential, to create life's coming attractions and a new trilogy. Pick up a good book and rest assured - you will set your mind free.

57. Magical M.A.N.T.R.A.: *How I use my voice IS a choice.*

Use your voice to empower others. Use it to shine light on goodness over and over again. And when you feel afraid to use it, be grateful to those who did - may they not have died in vain. Use your voice to tell a story about how you transformed in life through pain. And when you feel others try to silence you, make a choice to speak louder once again. Use your voice to speak up for others who don't have the privilege just the same. Use your voice to honor the evolutionary in you - it's your choice how you use it - to keep quiet is just insane.

58. Magical M.A.N.T.R.A.: I am a magical treasure hunter.

Imagine that - every day waking up with the mindset of the few. That great treasure is right around the corner, waiting there just for you. How fast then would you get up and jump out of bed? Looking forward to life rather than those things that you dread. From the time you open your eyes and your feet hit the floor, happiness is in sight and will bring what you adore. You'll be sure to receive clues from all sources around, all destined to bring you delight and turn up any frown. So, declare with me now before you take one more step. I am a magical treasure hunter, and that's a promise to be kept. Get out there and get ready, treasures appear without delay. Good people, fascinating places, and great experiences will complete your day.

9. Magical M.A.N.T.R.A.: *I am in the zone.*

    Focus is one of the key ingredients to getting things done, it's true. And, with this focus coupled with a plan and strong belief in self, then you have a good chance for the zone to come to you. The zone is where you dissociate from any distracting elements and allow the forward moving energy of achievement to flow. In this state of easy concentration, your performance shines through, it's like a state of grace you know. Whether it involves a career, a relationship or a project of great innovation too, when you are in the zone and its flow it is cause for celebration for you.

60. Magical M.A.N.T.R.A.: *I believe in myself.*

Bring forth your beautiful music, like a violin weeps with joy. Bring forth your strong voice, like a leader develops from a girl or boy. Suffering in silence no longer, wondering if you venture forth will anyone hear. With growing confidence, you answer your call - and you will be amazing my dear. Belief in yourself means having faith in your own gifts and ability. Belief in yourself helps to overcome doubt so you can see your possibility. Express yourself through the lens of believing, success in life you'll be receiving. It all starts in the mind, magical wonderment you will be achieving.

To my Butterflies:

Change calls for new traditions and rituals. I believe in every challenge there lies opportunity. So, when my nephew Patrick's graduation ceremony in person was canceled due to COVID-19, my family came together and presented him with speeches of our own. My message is for you as well.

My Keynote Speech for Pat "the Golden Eagle":

Now that you have done the work and have clarity around your purpose and calling, I'm going to give you some extra wisdom that I have learned to put in your B.A.G. as you set off on your new adventure to do epic stuff.

B*
Belief in yourself - you know who you are and are confident in your abilities - as long as you believe in yourself, no one will ever make you feel inferior.
Brilliant mind - you are blessed with good genes and intellect, now get curious about the world beyond - pay attention, get excited and tell all about it.
Betterment - you are only in competition with who you were yesterday - time to collaborate with others and become an even better version of yourself.

A*
Alignment - you have chosen amazing people to share this journey, trust your intuition and follow your moral compass welcoming synchronicities along the way.
Attitude - you created your mantra "Yes you Scan" – while we all have fears don't let them stop you (unless a bear is chasing you – then run)
Agape - you were created from unconditional love and my hope is that you continue spreading the same ("the highest form of love, charity")

G*
Generosity - you are blessed now go forth and be of service to your world.
Gratitude - my favorite - do your best to have an attitude of gratitude for your blessings, family who gave you roots and friends who have supported you along the way.
Grammie - you have angels beyond the veil who are going to protect you.

So, there you have it, now go forth and set the world on fire. I am so proud of you - time to inspire!

I Love You,

Meg

*6**1. Magical M.A.N.T.R.A.: I am healing by loving others.*

***"Healing yourself is connected with healing of others."* Yoko Ono, peace activist.**

After an individual hearing many years ago, I wanted to tell a teenage witness how impressive she was - so... I put my own fears aside that she wouldn't want to hear what I'd say. I asked her mother first if it was even okay. Her mother nodded and then stepped aside. I looked at this young girl and smiled with pride. "You are beautiful you know - both inside and out. Don't listen to the negativity from others." This point, I wanted to shout. "You have so many wonderful things that you will do in your life. You may not know this now - you'll make a difference because of your strife." I told her what I wish someone would have said to me. "I believe in you," I finished hoping to set both of our hearts free.

Something in my soul healed completely on that day, I keep reminding myself "I am healing by loving others - and somehow the world is better that way."

62. Magical M.A.N.T.R.A.: *I am enthusiastic about my journey.*

These are four wonderful words to empower your journey: vision, purpose, faith and gratitude. As long as you have a vision in your mind that matches your purpose, you can be enthusiastic about the unfolding ahead. As long as you have faith in that vision and your life's calling, you can trust that everything that unfolds will be an answer to your request. And, as long as you are grateful for all of your gifts that come from that vision, then you will be able to recognize the blessings you receive. Implementing the tools that are consistent with these four wonderful words, then you will be shouting in no time—I am enthusiastic about my journey as you look for the magic to come.

3. Magical M.A.N.T.R.A.: Remember who you are.

Whatever you do, don't let darkness overcome the light within you - remember who you are! Ruth Bader Ginsberg, a "Shero" passed away. You think how is it possible that the champions die yet the scourges of humanity stay. Maya Angelou said, "when people show you who they are believe them." This statement seems to cut both ways. You know many good people you love who just don't see current events the same way. What can you do, you fall to your knees and pray. Then you saw this quote from RBG and here she does say, "Fight for things that you care about, but do it in a way that will lead others to join you." Hip-Hip-Hooray! We need to come together - as one nation - it's the only way. Become leaders who heal and stand for good, we surely can slay! Engage the conversation as a human race and call out the power play. Don't let darkness overcome our light - we are the U.S. of A. You swear you will shine brighter and do what you can to help guide the way. Only then what is to come can be a better day!

6. 4. Magical M.A.N.T.R.A.: *I am strong, I never know who I am inspiring.*

I am strong. Say it again! Strength is an amazing word. It comes in many different forms. There is moral strength that comes from solid values and integrity. There is mental power that comes from clearing out the clutter through focus and meditation. There is physical strength that comes from taking care of and fueling your body. And, there is a vulnerable strength admitting you need help when the chips are down. So, say you are strong - in any respect it is a superpower. And, if you show up this way - you never know who you are inspiring to be strong too.

65. Magical M.A.N.T.R.A.: *I follow the divine to embrace love.*

Love is the force that moves mountains. Love is the key to create positive change. Love brings hope to this world as a powerful fountain. Love delivers joy. We are strengthened in the exchange. Love is the most important thing to begin with. Love one another may you embrace. Those words are said by Jesus, revolutionary teacher, and will in fact one day save the human race. That is the good energy that you talk about - an energy that will serve you throughout time. You will follow that energy of love as you follow the divine. Say, "I love you." Pass it on to one person and then another. In the end it is true, we are all sisters and we are all brothers.

6. Magical M.A.N.T.R.A.: *I choose to take care of myself.*

Be kind, be gentle, be loving, be true - to yourself. Self-care is so important especially during challenging times. If you are kind and gentle to yourself than it will be easier to be that way for others. Life can be very stressful. There is no way around that. And, deadlines to meet other people's priorities and expectations can be very taxing on your system There is a Zen proverb that is really good advice for those who find themselves weighed down by life. It goes as follows, "You should sit in meditation for twenty minutes every day - unless you're too busy; then you should sit for an hour." Give yourself the greatest gift by taking time to pay attention to how you feel. Give yourself at least 20 minutes of love and choose to take care of yourself. When the plane is about to go down, you have to put the oxygen on yourself first.

Receive

'grow through what you go through'

SECTION III. TELL ALL ABOUT IT

"The privilege of a lifetime is being who you are."
Joseph Campbell, American author, 1904-1987.

67. Magical M.A.N.T.R.A.: *I live from an abundance mindset.*

Would you rather choose a lack or abundance mentality? On the one side lack imprisons you, on the other abundance sets you free. One encourages thinking small grounded in scarcity too. The other challenges you to think big and stand tall, that a life of rich fulfillment is waiting for you. On the one hand, a mindset of resentment and fear that there will never be enough; on the other a mindset of happiness and possibility when the going really gets tough. Would you rather look at life as a know-it-all or would you rather process further learning so you can get help up after you fall? Remember that this is your once around, a one-time unfolding that you know to be true. Declare to live from an abundance mindset, with inspired action your abundance will shine the way for you.

8. Magical M.A.N.T.R.A.: *I surrender to joy.*

Is it life that you fear? How can that be? Life is supposed to be so extraordinary. Yes, there will be challenges and overwhelmingly hard times too. But, today did you see the colorful sunshine in the clouds shine through? Yes, after the darkness of the cocoon and the butterfly emerges, there is hope. From the sadness of loss and disappointment, there are joyful ways to help you cope. You surrender to joy, you are courageous and brave. Your journey awaits, to misery you are no slave. You surrender to joy, in a confusing world this still can be. You set aside your fear and look for as much magic and beauty.

9. Magical M.A.N.T.R.A.: *I embrace simplicity with a K.I.S.S.*

Set out Keep It Simple Sunshine. As far as acronyms go, turns into a K.I.S.S. - pure simplicity, I know. A touch on the lips or cheek as a sign of love and of reverence. It shows mutual care and concern, filled with so much benevolence. Everyone is challenged with issues, that is part of the human deliverance. It is how we help and take care of each other that makes all the difference. Let's keep it simple sunshine, right from the start. The way we begin must emanate from your delightful heart. I embrace simplicity with a K.I.S.S. and as far as we know. This builds a foundation for unconditional love to grow and grow and grow.

70. Magical M.A.N.T.R.A.: I choose to be a little creatively insane.

In *Alice in Wonderland*, Alice puts things in perspective when the Mad Hatter asks, "Have I gone mad?" She replied, "I'm afraid so. You're entirely bonkers. But I'll tell you a secret, all the best people are." The reality in her statement is that there is uniqueness in thinking outside the box. It can only make you better. There is such creativity in believing in the unbelievable. This concept is time-honored and true. Choosing to be a little creatively insane, is really quite good for you. There is no right or wrong direction in life, it is listening to the magic in your calling that will do. When we are delving into the realm of possibility, truth be told step out of a mold and be creatively you (with a touch of magical insanity too!)

71. Magical M.A.N.T.R.A.: I give myself permission to dream big.

It is time to give yourself permission to dream again, great anticipation of what is to come for you. When you move from visualizing to a grand reality, excitement is the key ingredient that creates an incredible brew. Expect the unexpected, through your magical intentions and process too. With your role as the master magician, incredible delight is waiting for you. Dream big, bigger, biggest, you will inspire even the most formidable skeptics. No longer content with mere mediocrity, the greatest dreamers are not apoplectic. Get out of the box and give yourself permission to learn to dream again, just think how this shift will work out for you - always better to dream in the end.

72. Magical M.A.N.T.R.A.: *I am a magical creative being.*

"Make believe you are brave and the trick will take you far. You may be as brave as you make believe you are..."

Rodgers & Hammerstein, lyrics from "Whistle a Happy Tune," *The King and I*, **American musical theater writing team.**

When telling your story, there is a delicate balance between baring your soul and finding a safe place to do so. For those of you who have tapped into your creative source, it no longer is acceptable to hold back. You must express what tugs at your heart. In fact, it may be deleterious to your very well being to turn your back on sharing what you have discovered. Yet, it remains a frightening task to undertake when exposing a cherished part of you for the world to see. You might say, "I must write - but what if it is ridiculed?" You might say, "I must sing - but what if they laugh?" There is a plethora of excuses you can use to hide, but how does that serve you? So be brave, sing, dance or express whatever modality moves you. Make believe you are a star. Seriously, only then will you be able go far.

To my Butterflies:

What kind of person do you want to be? Here is your examination of consciousness. As I am no stranger to the scholastic tests that are meant to clarify what one has learned after a course of study, this exam is utterly important too.

Sure, high school exams, college finals, master's comprehensives, even Bar exams are vital as they test your grasp on knowledge that will ultimately determine your expertise in an area. However, you are just spitting out what you have learned to get a degree or a license. This examination asks you to delve deeper - it asks you to decide what your impact on humanity will be.

Greed v. Kindness. Love v. Hate. Competition v. Collaboration. The Few v. The Many. I ask you to think critically as to what can unfold in your life on a smaller scale, magnified on a greater one. The question remains, which reality will you choose. And then, it follows, will you be proud of your answer?

As the actress Cynthia Nixon mentioned at the Tony Awards in 2017, "Eighty years ago, (Lillian Hellman) wrote, 'There are people who eat the earth and eat all the people on it, and other people who just stand around and watch them do it.' My love, my gratitude and my undying respect go out to all the people in 2017 who are refusing to just stand and watch them do it. Thank you."

So, I ask you the only question on your examination of consciousness – "What kind of person do you want to be?"

I Love You,

Meg

73. Magical M.A.N.T.R.A.: *I show up brave whatever life throws my way.*

Today, I want you to say, "I show up brave whatever life throws my way." You may not feel like this is possible, but I guarantee you'll be okay. Whatever life presents, there is a strength within that will come through. Tap right into your source, keep your head up and the mystery you'll undo. There are experiences you'll face, but you won't be alone on that ride. You'll be triumphant - put down those mountains carried, and walk with me side by side. There is strength in your brave spirit, even when you walk alone. Remember you have friends close by to support you, as long as you have a phone. So, you find yourself with these words, there are no mistakes in life, it's true. Show up brave, you incredible warrior, this message is just for you.

74. Magical M.A.N.T.R.A.: *I honor my feelings.*

It is very important to pay attention to your feelings; they are the conscious experience of your emotions from happiness to strife. When you tune in to your intuition as to how you feel on any given day, you bring more awareness to your life. And in return, you can be proactive to your surroundings and to others. You can truly know yourself better to make solid decisions whether a brother, sister, father or mother. You can get an accurate reading on what is going on inside your body too. You'll feel less vulnerable, even more confident to better honor your innermost you. Emotions of joy, sadness, anger, disgust and fear are all a part of the human psyche. They are there to guide, protect and empower - success is more likely. When you honor your feelings and take back your power, you'll navigate life better each hour by hour.

75. Magical M.A.N.T.R.A.: *I enjoy the magic of my journey.*

"A journey is like marriage. The certain way to be wrong is to think you can control it."
John Steinbeck, American author, 1902-1968.

There is magic when you release the need to control everything. There is actual freedom when you do what you can and step back to allow the universe to do its thing. When you try to control everything, you may miss out on something greater that awaits you. Just listen in this moment to the whispers of your soul as it calls out "stop, stop, stop - pay attention." Take a moment to get still on your magical journey to bliss and listen to the inner workings. You can actually experience the magic of what you have set into motion. You are in this moment at the exact place you are meant to be. Enjoying the magic of your journey.

76. Magical M.A.N.T.R.A.: *I meet cynicism and divisiveness with love.*

You may be an incredibly sensitive person. You may be deeply affected by what is going on all around you. When there seems to be a lot of anger, pain, sadness, suffering and most of all fear being passed around like a prize during challenging times, you may even want to hide. What to do when supposed leaders and individuals who stand before you offer their own brand of immorality that robs humans of their dignity? How do the defenders of the mystical and magical fight back against cynicism and divisiveness when it threatens to rule the day? Of course, you speak up for love. It's love, love, and more love! You connect with love. You shout out with love. And, you spread the love. That is the kind of magical thinking that will break through the fear and open up humanity to something better that you know is possible.

7. Magical M.A.N.T.R.A.: *I declutter what no longer serves me.*

It is good advice to conduct a physical and spiritual cleaning at least every six months. If you are reading this now, it just might be the perfect time. While removing unnecessary items from your physical closet when space is limited may be an obvious thing to do, it is the spiritual side of things that might be a bit harder for you. Getting rid of and donating items of clothes that are outdated or no longer fit, for the emotional clearing you will need extra time to sit. Take a piece of paper and figure out what you need to do. Write down all the stuff in your head that is really bothering you. Negative energy takes up too much space, going over and fine-tuning your relationship and your finances can give you much grace. At the end of your efforts, you might just feel lighter. Certainly, creating an inventory of your spiritual life, declutter the old stories and become a new chapter writer.

78. Magical M.A.N.T.R.A.: *I am the keeper of the light.*

Last night, I watched Gloria Steinman who at 80 was asked who she wanted to pass the torch to. She replied, "I'm keeping the torch, but going to use it to light up each and every torch of every woman or man I meet." THIS! This is what it is all about. Using your big beautiful light to help others to shine theirs too. These are the qualities of divine badass nurturers and creators. They step up and own their gifts in collaboration with others empowering them to use their voice for good. Have a conversation from this point of view. Keep your own power, shine your light and pass that on so others can too.

79. Magical M.A.N.T.R.A.: *I have faith in life as it unfolds before me.*

That which is in you impelling you forward is in the things and people you need, impelling them towards you." Wallace Wattles, American New Thought writer, 1860-1911.

The law of attraction says that you will attract into your life whatever you focus on. Whatever you give your energy and attention to, will eventually, like karma, come right back to you. In that respect, I have had the tremendous fortune to spend hours basking in wisdom with my dad. I like to think that I attract the inspiring conversations around consciousness with him that get my juices flowing. He is a brilliant man who not only is a seeker but a healer too. There is much to learn. I am lucky to be blessed with the DNA of both my parents. While he tends to be a bit too conservative and traditional, I challenge him too to see the goodness in the world from a different perspective. Together, we grow. Moment by moment I have learned that all of us attract what we put into life as the mystery unfolds before us. Leaving me with a sense that I must continue to show up doing my best and attract more of those good people there. As long as we follow our own bliss, those who are aligned will show up to engage the conversation, no doubt about that.

80. Magical M.A.N.T.R.A.: *I am in the business of relationships.*

You set out and have accomplished much. Finished what you started. You planted and nurtured many seeds, followed the path that you once charted. Above all else, you are most grateful for your friendships are such wonderful things. Your relationships that sustain you, the conversations that have given you wings. Putting yourself out there with great courage, surrounded by love that has seen you through. Every step of the way you know you are blessed because of magical people too. You may have faced loss and climbed mountains, the challenge of the experiences may have brought you to your knees. It's the energy of the people with you, that helps you sparkle and shine whenever you please. You may know something wonderful is about to happen, every time you realize a dream. Then what really gives your life meaning is the fact you are in the presence of queens. So place your tiara on your head, while you say this clearly too. "I am in the business of relationships," people who help all your wishes come true.

81. Magical M.A.N.T.R.A.: *I am fine, one day at a time.*

One day you're down, the next day you shine. One day you frown, the next day you feel fine. The news is overwhelmingly sad, then magnificently sublime. The best you can do is go one day at a time. Act with a clear head for sure. Examine possibilities as they come. Look at each and every door. With the wisdom you have, you'll choose the right one. If emotions overwhelm, then you'll give in to a good laugh or cry. But you'll never get stuck, if you give it the good college try. Take it one day at a time, begin with small steps and endure. It is true, life can be rough, for this there is no cure. Taking steps forward is always a solution, if you remember this all of what unfolds can be a part of your spiritual evolution.

82. Magical M.A.N.T.R.A.: *I am grateful for awareness.*

You may be grateful to be an observer of what unfolds around you. You may be grateful that you live in a society where free speech is a fundamental value. You may be grateful for the ability to express your opinion and views in an intelligent manner. You may be grateful that you were raised to know the value of the human spirit where positivity is your banner. You may be grateful for your tribe of magical ones and grateful for your family too. And you may be grateful for the courage of your convictions. You may be grateful for the something wonderful that will pull you through. You may be grateful that you know your calling to inspire and help others to shine. And, you may be grateful for all the awareness above upon which to build a world mirrored in the divine.

To my Butterflies:

This letter to you asks one favor: please stop and think before you drink the proverbial Kool-Aid.

Why is it a "thing" that mass amounts of people willingly give the power of their own qualified consciousness away? Historically, society screws itself when it gives one person or one ideology the power to control the masses. I know that I don't follow clowns around town who tell me to hate another person because of what they look like. I'm not going to agree with a religion that does not practice the love it intends to preach. I don't drink the Kool-Aid and ask please neither should any of you.

Question authority - don't defer because of a title. Be a part of a solution-based world, seeking a vision of connection where collaborative efforts benefit a broader group. Turn away those who mock our precious institutions rather than improve upon them. You really do get to choose. You are a thinking person - let's all start acting like it!

Listen more, talk less. Love more, argue less. Hope more, fear less. Relax more, worry less. Believe more, doubt less. Play more, work less.

I Love You,

Meg

83. Magical M.A.N.T.R.A.: I believed I could, so I did.

Set your intention. Go ahead it's all you. Before you set off on your next adventure, it is important to get a clue. There is a power in your desires, visualize well your strategy too. And then put it all into action, all because you know what you can do. The journey begins with your first step, but the plan unfolds all along. Your voice will be heard for eternity as long as you never give up, that'd be wrong. And, for sure as you move forward, you will be marching to your own beautiful song. You will finally get to your destination, paying attention to all the messages it holds. I believed I could, so I did will be your melody. A story of perseverance that continues to unfold.

4. Magical M.A.N.T.R.A.: *I have an abundance of faith.*

In the midst of this darkness, each one of us must light our candle. Trust is something that we all need to work towards again if we are to coexist in a respectful and peaceful way. There is so much disdain and manipulation going on it is overwhelming. More than ever we need faith. A confidence in what we hope for, a renewal of what we believe we could. When others attempt to destroy the fabric of decency, faith is the challenge to do good. Faith will help us hold up this perfect union to the highest standards even though we are all perfectly flawed. An abundance of faith with inspired action will not let hate overtake us, we will rest joy from evil's claws. We can build a future together, we surely can pave the way. No more pandering to the worst part of each of us, have faith our joint light will save the day.

5. Magical M.A.N.T.R.A.: *I live a virtuous life.*

All around the world, you'll find different people and their amazing traditions. One thing stands the test of time, throughout most cultures there is this one underlying vision. There are basic virtues all humanity must cling to if we are ever to reach the divine. Aristotle, the Greek philosopher (384-322 BC), knew this as he spoke about *eudaimonia* and taught in his time. He spoke about well-being and laid out these 12 virtues to get the people there. They are courage, temperance, liberality, magnificence, and generous care. Ambition, patience, friendliness, truthfulness, wit, modesty too. And, the final one he spoke about was justice for me and you.

6. Magical M.A.N.T.R.A.: *I know humanity is my race and love is my religion.*

Our children are watching us. What kind of legacy shall we leave to them. This is so much bigger than our anger or disgust. It is an opportunity to show the world what kind of nation we are at our core. The U.S. Constitution stands as an example for other countries to strive for better. The Statue of Liberty is a symbol to the world of acceptance of humanity in all its various colors, and beliefs. "We the People" declares our independence as a nation of laws against tyranny. Let this American experiment be guided by a peaceful transition to move forward together. We need to be responsible citizens of the world and remember that this is not just about us. Keep that in mind as we are tempted to judge each other. We all have our reasons; we all want to be heard and validated. Most importantly, we all want to keep hope alive. For this dream, we cannot remain silent.

87. Magical M.A.N.T.R.A.: *I am going to shine my light so bright.*

You are different right now than you were one year ago, last week, or even earlier today. You must remember the lessons that you've learned along the way. As you continue on your journey to bliss, let that transformative evolution be your guide. With the potential of changing the world for the better, take a deep breath and let go from deep inside. The brighter you shine, the greater you'll illuminate the darkness. Trust the process divine so you can bring color to the starkness. Until the day arrived when the beautiful butterfly broke free, say out loud, now I am going to shine my light so bright for the world to see.

8. Magical M.A.N.T.R.A.: *I choose me, now I'm free.*

If today you are questioning how to send the blahs away, start with this mantra and get ready! It's time to begin to play. Stop thinking what others would want to say to you. Instead choose to live your life finding happiness in what you do. Enough is enough. This is your life, it is time to believe in your path. Say out loud, I choose me, now I'm free. That's your currency, you know how to do the math. Waking up to discover the freedom that you see, it's unselfish to finally allow your heart to feel its glee. So do yourself a favor, set your boundaries for other to see. Set out the course on great purpose, empower yourself to be free. You choose, you say, you stand up for you. For if you don't, no one will for you.

89. Magical M.A.N.T.R.A.: *I am spiritually awake.*

I often pray at the end of my days, when I meet my maker, I'll have this to say:

I did my best to show up and not judge what I didn't understand. I spoke up consistently for love, at least that was my great plan. I stood up to the smallness of those in power who heralded from a place of greed. And I asked forgiveness for my own missteps, and righted my moral compass to help me lead. I opened my mind to new perspectives from the many and the few. I did not let stress overwhelm me, I did my best to have no regrets too. I spoke up for truth and justice. And from my heart space, I did not stray. I did challenge myself out of my comfort zone, and with gratitude, discovered bliss along the way. I am spiritually awake.

90. Magical M.A.N.T.R.A.: *I am becoming perfectly.*

Becoming is an amazing notion. The dictionary defines it as to begin to be. Not to do, but to be everything that actually is meant to unfold effortlessly. Do you think that everything becoming starts from divine synchronicity? Well if you remain conscious, you'll witness the acorn ultimately become a tree. All in all, you may start out hoping for one thing but life delivers another. Fundamental change happens there, the perfect results you'll discover. How you show up now is one thing that is going to set you free. Your becoming is your gift to God - the universal divine energy. And my friends, let it be said that you are becoming perfectly.

9 1. **Magical M.A.N.T.R.A.: *I let go into the effortless flow.***

Let go into the effortless flow. Some call the flow loving energy and others divine. It doesn't matter what you label it, when you release resistance it will feel so sublime. Imagine being carried up and away, rising higher and higher to a better perspective to see your new day. When you allow the hot air to lift you rather than weighing you down, you will effortlessly be carried all around. Soaring with the eagles, rather improves upon your view. A magnificence only seen, if you know what to do. I imagine that is what a butterfly must feel for the first time it uses its wings. A trust in creation even if scared and overwhelmed by many things. This flow of life filled with amazing surprises, doing what you can then letting go truly revitalizes.

2. Magical M.A.N.T.R.A.: *I matter and can change the world for the better.*

You may not think that you can change the world - think again. You may be that one small change in your little corner that has ripple effects of wonder all across the globe. Just one act of kindness, making another aware of injustice. Just one thing that gives hope in a world full of hopelessness. Just adding a little more joy to another person's day. That is what you must keep in mind as you travel on this journey. You matter. Remember, you can change the world for the better. This affirmation will be sure to empower the greatest revolution of love yet to be seen.

93. Magical M.A.N.T.R.A.: *I am bolstered by amazing and inspiring stories.*

Whenever doubt creeps in and threatens to hi-jack your confidence, think about this. There are so many people who can inspire you. Bolstered by this, those who share stories of vulnerability shine through. For instance, there are those underdogs who never had a chance. They never gave up and eventually showed up to lead the dance. It is the story of the individuals who defy all odds to persevere. It is the tale of the miraculous that makes one smile from ear to ear. Staying hopeful is never easy, but let me tell you this much is true. When you sit and hear amazing and inspiring stories, you get goosebumps and know what you need to do. Keep moving forward, don't give up for you'll be convinced you are wonderful too.

94. Magical M.A.N.T.R.A.: I have a magical imagination.

John Lennon wrote the lyrics, "Imagine all the people living life in peace." Just thinking of that, the likelihood does in fact increase. Because you may be a dreamer, you are encouraged to dwell in possibility too. In your magical imagination, there's a vision that readily comes through. May peace prevail on Earth, it is time for the collective consciousness to believe. Go in that direction of peace and that is just what you may receive. Imagine a world where actions give rise to love not despair or baseless acts. Evil is real, but LOVE is stronger - those are the facts. Imagine, if you can dream it, you can do it - please persist! Take your control back and only then a new reality can exist. In your magical imagination, amazing things start to happen there. Therein lies a greater peace and it is waiting, and for that stand up and cheer.

95. Magical M.A.N.T.R.A.: *I know that sometimes the best ideas come heaven sent.*

Inspired thought breeds inspired action. The seeds planted gives rise to a creativity that brings great joy to the world. Where does it come from you may ask? Well what if it came heaven sent. Little sparks of magic sprinkled from above brought to life with great awareness and love. What are those ideas that are calling to you? Whispering here - let's go for an adventure and see it through. Why not accept the invitation and take a risk? Might lead you down a road that you can't believe actually exists. If magic and miracles are the gift of today, believe in what you receive and let it light up the way. Intuition to guide you and a little magical pixie dust too, know that the best ideas come heaven sent delivered straight to you.

6. Magical M.A.N.T.R.A.: *I connect to my colorful soul.*

I connect to my colorful soul. When I do, the whole world lights up and I am closer to my goal. Of a more beautiful place filled with wonder and jaw dropping scenes, a creator's delight and an art lover's dream. Like the colors of a rainbow, my spirit shines right through. Highlighted by shades of red, orange, yellow, green, violet and blue. Connecting within, I'm bound to go on a colorful adventure I will treasure. Follow my own colorful road, rejoicing in a beauty beyond measure.

7. Magical M.A.N.T.R.A.: *I dream big and default to a miraculous mindset.*

That is it - you create a life of big dreams. One that will lead towards greater self-esteem. Just accept who you are on any given day. This is all about the miraculous mindset - through uplifting contemplation it will keep your nasty triggers away. You know some days there will be negative push back. That little voice in your head telling you that you're no good. These are the challenges you will face, but be sure that awareness is for the good. Life will bring you many surprises, some wonderful and some not so nice. But to create a habit in this miraculous mindset, you'll be offered the following advice. Start your day with beautiful intentions. Fill your mind with powerful dreams. Connect from a place of possibility - meditate on magical things.

8. Magical M.A.N.T.R.A.: *I don't forget to get my Vitamin SEA.*

The ocean can be your happy place. To see the clear blue sky, to feel the breeze on your face, to hear the crashing of the waves, and to taste the salty sea. When you go to that place in person or in your mind, your soul can feel amazingly free. The ocean can be your happy place; it can cure your anxiety. You can close your eyes and visualize, you can feel a sense of peace - such a treat. The ocean can be your happy place. In the water you can be baptized and renewed, while the sand massages your tired feet. The sun's warmth nourishes your skin, that's where you can get your vitamin SEA. Go there in your mind - and it's a promise, you'll find - empowered you will be.

9. Magical M.A.N.T.R.A.: *I choose the greatest of all virtues – love.*

With awareness of what unfolds, we are not tempted by streets of gold. We watch our world cry out so bold - to do what can be done in light of what we behold. We're scared at times to be trolled. We know those who are in power for greed keep it if we fold. We know love will save us, our courageous souls can't be sold. Faith begins at the end of understanding - of this we are told. Run from the hate of false prophets. Time to take off our blindfold. Embrace love and light, and choose the greatest virtues of old. For love tells a better story and there we can experience a happiness extolled.

To my Butterflies:

Sending out a call for leaders today!

I am ready to start a conversation of strength, dignity, honor, mutual respect and service. Yes, there will always be challenges on this historical journey. Yes, there will always be those who protect their own self interests. I am looking for the visionaries of the world to step up and engage the conversation from a patriotic notion of wonderful possibility.

Not all people in leadership positions deserve to be leaders; the power grab can go to the head of those who possess a weak character. But not you, you fight for one world and the pursuit of happiness too. In the Broadway show Hamilton, written by Lin Manuela Miranda, the cast of characters sang, "who lives, who dies, who tells your story?" Quite a powerful refrain.

This is where a part of me opened up. This is where I changed. I understood that we all are responsible for keeping the dream and promise of a vision of a greatness alive as citizens of the world. This is where I realized I am a leader writing my story side by side with you for worthy gains.

How do we want to be remembered in the history books in this land of the free, the home of the brave? Black, white, women, men, gay, straight - each person doing their best to contribute to the promise. I know these truths that formed the basis of America to be self-evident - this is a good place to be. Many come far and wide in search of the American Dream. Many would do anything to defend what our forefathers began. Many have worked tirelessly to improve upon the foundation of the principles in our living and breathing Constitution. It is time to lead from here - to receive what is good in the world to heal the pain. Be a leader to that end!

I Love You,

Meg

Get Ready
What are you waiting for?

If nothing ever changed, there'd be no butterflies.

SECTION IV. TIME TO SPARKLE AND SHINE

"Adopt the pace of nature: her secret is patience."
Ralph Waldo Emerson, American poet, 1803-1882

100. Magical M.A.N.T.R.A.: *I set my own pace to gain clarity.*

Ok, so you say, "everything I desire is there waiting for me. Everything I have prepared for is about to unfold to help me run free. And of course, I understand what I seek is seeking me, but I can't catch my breath - how will I be able to see. I feel overwhelmed if truth be told, it is starting to feel like a bill of goods I have been sold." Stop then, if you are not sure that you will enjoy the rewards of what you sow. If you are so tired, it is okay to rest and rejuvenate a little longer before you press go. YES! This is not a race to check off the things you place on your list. This is your life, one moment at a time. And, it's important to take a break, so don't resist. Self-care is so vital. You intuitively know what is best. Go at your own pace. In addition to the external world, focus on your internal world and decompress. Get in touch with your body and your soul. Figure out what you need, then rock n' roll. If your mind is a bit cluttered, take a time-out to get clarity. Be patient and mindful, this time to reconnect is a form of charity. Then, when you are bright and shiny after reengaging with you, bring it on universe - together you'll know what to do.

1 01. Magical M.A.N.T.R.A.: Keep going - beautiful ones, we got this.

Whilst external forces engender stirrings in your soul, it's time to act to be truly intentional in your role. Especially if health, prosperity and goodness is your goal, beautiful one stress will take its toll. In furtherance of the highest good, start moving in incremental steps. At a pace you can handle, you will experience greatness and its effects. Set an intention, BELIEVE, and with tremendous gratitude start writing a better story. On your secret scroll of life, therein lies the glory. Keep going, we've got this.

102. Magical M.A.N.T.R.A.: *I shine my light and enjoy what the universe offers.*

There are people, experiences and things in life that threaten to dim your light. Words said that hurt you. People's action that attempt to belittle you. And, nastiness that is used in hopes to quiet or control you. Instead of falling prey or buckling under the pressure, truly love who you are, ignore them and show up for yourself anyway. You can use the energy of others, either positive or negative, as fuel to shine away. So just for today, in this time, in this place, choose to shine the beauty and enjoy the moments that the universe offers in each moment. And just watch as the naysayers with their lower vibration just diminish and go away. May you see beyond the veil of what society wants you to believe is true and embrace your beautiful truth, built on your beautiful dreams, designed for beautiful YOU.

To my Butterflies:

What are you waiting for? If it is permission you seek to move forward, it is yours. Don't waste your time engaging in unnecessary drama playing other people's silly games. They have their own rules, and unfortunately if they choose, at a moment's notice these rules can always change. You will find that it will never be enough, just don't show up and take the blame. Change your perspective now so you won't go insane.

What do you think will happen when you set your own boundaries and play your own game? I would surmise that there is only one governing rule to guide you and the *Golden Rule* is its name. When you start to live your life loving others guided by your heart, no one will have power over you, so don't even start.

Assume the feeling of your own life wishes and goals fulfilled and stay true to the path that unfolds. Break out of the imaginary box, do your best and do what ultimately makes you happy - never be sold. Time here is short, you will only regret what you do not do. And remember if you are fooled into playing silly games, the joke is really on you. You are not a puppet, so don't act like one. The only question at the end of the day is for you to answer - have you set a sound legacy by following your bliss. The final results will unfold over your lifetime - so have fun. Class dismissed.

I Love You,

Meg

103. Magical M.A.N.T.R.A.: *Be impeccable with what follows the great I AM.*

Want to empower your life - start here!
I am healthy
I am happy
I am loved
I am beautiful
I am strong
I am a success
I am authentically me
Everything happens for a reason, everything works out for me
I expect magic and miracles
I am grateful
Something wonderful is about to happen!

104. *Magical M.A.N.T.R.A.: Instead of going negative, I get curious.*

One of the most interesting things about life is that when we are so consumed by a dark place, we forget that we can be the light. Change begins when we go within. That dark transformation of the caterpillar can be so scary. We may at times feel alone and hopeless, but there is growth to the natural process that allows us to break through and bring others along. When we feel shattered when we fall, we forget that we can take our broken pieces and rearrange them into someone even more beautiful. We are stronger when we lift each other up to help the broken parts heal. We have lived this and still do every day when we all share our light. Instead of going negative, get curious as to what we can become together.

105. Magical M.A.N.T.R.A.: I choose to spread love.

"I went inside my heart to see how it was. Something there makes me hear the whole world weeping." **Rumi**, 13th century Persian poet, 1207-1273.

Those challenging events we thought we could handle in a vacuum can pile up, testing our resolve. It may seem like those who lead with a message of love and courage perish while the toxic ones that spew hate still remain. The question we may want to ask now is how do we return to joy. And in the midst of our contemplation, we receive messages from unlikely sources, my friend Nora Olaso said (translated from Spanish) "God who can do everything, created us with the ability to love in such profound ways that we are not able to imagine, because in that depth we find him and it is then that all our fears disappear. Everything we do has to be for the sake of others - intentionally." So, we get to choose, in the midst of darkness, what we want to do. We can turn our light on or not. We can spread love or not. And, we can tell those we love what they mean to us today, for tomorrow is promised to no one.

106. Magical M.A.N.T.R.A.: *I get to choose.*

You may be weary of people who peddle their wares in fear. The magnanimous "they" want you to close your eyes and listen to what they say. They want you to trust them to make decisions for you - for they want you to believe that is in your "best interest" to follow what they say and do. To that open your eyes even bigger, get curious as to what they don't want you to see. With critical thinking and awareness, you know what is right in front of you to see. You get to choose where your energy goes. You are an intelligent being and look to see the facts right under your nose. You do your best to examine triggers and fears when they rise up, so you can choose the next courageous step and not give up. To empower a collective consciousness founded in good, love and trust, you get to choose what you want to manifest and adjust. Turn off the noise, the lies and vitriol, disgust too - as a smart cookie, you know what you want for you. Today is the time to hold yourself accountable to change, to that end, may you find peace in the exchange.

107. Magical M.A.N.T.R.A.: I choose love over fear and all the obstacles disappear.

Choose love. The energy is definitely more playful than fear. With love, you collaborate more. With love, you dance more. With love, you get things done. Prioritize your life - set out a strategy for success - put it down on paper and ask the universe to deliver the rest. If you let fear take over, your blinders go up and you are unable to see. Open your eyes, help is there that is always waiting to set you free. More love, more play and go out there in spite of your fear. Lo and behold any obstacles just begin to disappear.

108. Magical M.A.N.T.R.A.: *I get ready to be ready.*

You may have wanted to go up in a hot air balloon. In fact, you may plan to in Paris one day flying high above the Eiffel Tower and its city of lights. You're so ready to go - in your mind you have already taken the trip and the feeling is no less than magical. You may have already experienced what you have set out in your mind. You see who is there with you, you may feel wonderful in your own skin and you are empowered by the celebration. It doesn't matter that you still may not be ready to go now - you are getting ready to be ready when the world is open and the circumstances allow. So, visualize what you want to do, who you want to be, and how you want to feel. In your life, when you go there in the mind, the body will follow and it will be real. Evidence shows the path will light up when the pieces come together. You will truly be there about to take flight empowered by a gentle breeze in any kind of weather.

To my Butterflies:

Sparkle & Shine - the Finale
Trust, count to three and set your magical wishes free.

Every August, inspired by my friend and author of *E-Squared*, Pam Grout, I write my wishes in the sand under the full moon.

My ultimate wish is for world peace.
Inspired by the sea, I set out my thoughts succinctly:

"When I'm really old and grey
I pray my mind is invaded by beautiful memories.
Of a life well lived and continues to be
One where I allowed the law of attraction to deliver to me
Health, love, connections and prosperity.
For stress dissipates when passion within is set free
A life of no regrets and where my mind's eye can see.
My purpose unfolds as it continues to call to me
Go where you are loved to serve founded in generosity.
All the faces I've known, the souls that gave me much glee
And when I seek peace - I'll sit by the beautiful sea.
Facing the ocean
I write wishes in the sand with words of clarity.
I'll worship at the hand of gratitude for the kindness presented to me
My blessings foretold when I came as a small baby.
My spirit courageously sings aloud a beautiful legacy
I take my place beside the waves and clouds for what feels like eternity.
Surrounded by my circle of angels
There I know I am truly blessed and am so very happy."

I Love You.

Get Ready to Dazzle - I Believe in You!

Meg

EPILOGUE

"I dwell in possibility." **Emily Dickinson, American poet, 1830-1886.**

---

*N*ow, I am ready for a wonderful adventure. I suppose this feeling has been coming on for quite some time. New Beginnings. Time to start manifesting amazing people, places and things effortlessly. Cleaned out some clutter, opened up some sacred space that allows me to see clearly in front of me. And, now is the best time to align with the higher vibration of the universe after a bit of a rocky start. With each M.A.N.T.R.A., I affirm and create a practice that gives way to an opening into the spiritual swoosh!

Do you know what the spiritual swoosh is?

Ever see the 2003 computer-animated adventure film produced by Pixar Animation Studios and released by Walt Disney Pictures called *Finding Nemo*? It tells the story of an overprotective clownfish named Marlin, who along with a regal blue tang Dory searches for his missing son Nemo. There is a scene when Marlin and Dori are with the lovable surfer-dude turtle named Crush looking for a way to get to Sydney, Australia quickly to rescue Nemo. Crush encourages Dori and Marlin to jump into the East Australia Current, the EAC, and ride it effortlessly to their destination. Looking from the outside-in, it seemed almost impossible for them to take a leap of faith and jump because everything and everyone was going by so quickly. Then, all of a sudden, there was that right moment - time stood still and the opportunity opened up to be brave and courageous. They must make the split-second decision to go or miss their chance. When they do, everything falls into place and it feels like a great big push from the universe - a spiritual swooooossshhh!

In your life, everything that has happened on the journey has led you to this moment in time. Perseverance and a never give up attitude have brought you farther than you could even imagine at the outset. You are so ready today for what life has to offer having benefitted from all the experiences and lessons. Now, after 108 M.A.N.T.R.A.s, the circle is complete and you hopefully are more open and willing to keep moving forward looking to effortlessly jump into the spiritual swoosh and the ride of your life. You might feel a trust and faith beyond measure now that positive neural pathways have been created. With patience and following your intuition as to what the next best step is, timing is on your side. Gathering all the clues, the mystery unfolds as you laugh with delight recognizing synchronicities in this universe welcoming you into the effortless flow.

You honor the fact that you may have had to hit rock bottom to get there, perhaps losing what you believe was everything at the time. Now the veil has lifted, the obstacles move out of your way, you find an entry place and the next great adventure begins. How amazing it is that you took the time to set out a new practice in your life that has you seeing the opportunity in that new day. And sometimes, even when you don't have the courage or energy to jump in yourself, you are willing to ask for help from an angel, soul sister or another butterfly who will grab you by the hand and take you with them as the wind swooshes under your budding wings to carry you away. Now that you asked, believed and received - paid attention, got astonished and are ready to tell all about it, your spirit is ready to sparkle & shine - happy swooshing as you attract and manifest from a higher vibration my Butterflies. I cannot wait to meet you there and play!

ACKNOWLEDGMENTS

This book of affirmations is a part of my healing process and a labor of love that began in 2016. After I published my first book, *The Magical Guide to Bliss (MGTB)*, I followed this guide that led me on a journey to both write this handbook of tools along with finishing up my memoir entitled *Butterfly Awakens*. I incorporated a daily affirmation practice that could go along with MGTB's Insights of the Day and the Magical Keys to Bliss. Evolving over time, it became another favorite writing practice that helped me to start each day from a place of positivity that I got to share with others. I am profoundly grateful for all of those beautiful people on Facebook and Instagram who responded to my work and kept me inspired to continue writing.

To begin, I am grateful to my cousin Margaret Santangelo for being a constant inspiration on my writing journey. For Matt Kovachy, for coining the term "MEG"nets that has led to "MEG"net Affirmation Cards to Attract Positive Vibes that is as an accompaniment to this book. I am grateful to Dr. Jessica Mosley for her enduring friendship, for the incredible publicity that has built the foundation for my business and for her assistance publishing this book. And, especially for the beautiful sparkly, butterfly artwork of Kim Anderson. You brought this book to life with your colorful images and made it truly *Sparkle & Shine*.

I want to thank my family for supporting my dreams - Frank, Michael, Ava, Mary and the Scanlons, Aimee and the Lewises and my dad, Dr. Michael Nocero Jr., the Poppie. I am grateful to my Butterflies whose creative magical spirits complete my circle. Specifically, Coco Padilla, Lisa Lommerin, Alicia Eliscu, Michele Barrett, Grace Hawley, Teda Melero, Denise Lane, Priscilla Dawkins, S.I.S., Grissel Seijo, Francisca Phillips, Pau de Regil, Norma de Regil, Mari Teresa Andrechuk (and the statue of Virgin Mary in the box), Corin Sands, Mari Vina Rodriguez, Jessica Quesada, Janet Woods, Hector Prado, Pam Grout, Amy Butler, Lily Shea Woods, Tanya Mikaela, Giseli & Kevin Lemay, Dr. Delene Musielak, Mike Spatola, Kellie Santos de Jesus, Berta Medina, Dr. Ceci Shaw, Dr. Eva Paglialonga, Maite Albuerne, Andrew Deutsch, Sandra Echevarria, Shelley Roxanne, Payton Sorenson, Frank Dailey, Pat Santangelo, Betty Santangelo, Eileen

Hult, Charles Santangelo, Aaliyah Taylor, Judy Echavez, Randee Lehrer, Pamela Kohl, Richard Jurgens, Michele Drucker, my prayer group, my Camino Amigos and my Butterfly Circle.

But most of all, I want to thank the children's author Theodor Seuss Geisel, or more commonly known as Dr. Seuss. His anapestic tetrameter, a poetic meter employed by many poets of the English literary canon, inspired me as I created my insights and rhymes. For Dr. Seuss's subtle delivery of profound wisdom against the moral dilemmas in this world, I am grateful for his books, his divine influence on my writing and the beautiful messages delivered so well.

In his honor, I will leave you with this Dr. Seuss quote from *Oh, the Places You'll Go!*:

"Kid, you'll move mountains! You're off to great places. Today is your day! Your mountain is waiting. So... get on your way!"

Fly Butterflies Fly - you will never know what you are capable of if you do not try.

It's Time to Manifest the Life of Your Dreams!

I Love You,

Meg

ABOUT THE AUTHOR

Meg Nocero, Esq. is an attorney, an inspirational speaker, ICF certified empowerment coach and award-winning author of *The Magical Guide to Bliss, Daily Keys to Unlock Your Dreams, Spirit & Inner Bliss*. She holds a B.A. in Spanish, with a concentration in Italian from Boston College; a M.A. in International Affairs from the University of Miami; and a J.D. from St. Thomas University School of Law. Ms. Nocero is the owner of Butterflies & Bliss, LLC, founded a non-profit called S.H.I.N.E. Networking Inc. that provides educational scholarships to young innovative leaders and recognizes leaders in her community with *Taz Grout* Good Neighbor Award, and is a Love Button Global Movement Ambassador.

She received a certificate in the Science of Wellbeing from Yale University and a Certificate in Happiness Studies through Harvard Professor Dr. Tal Ben-Shahar's Happiness Studies Academy. She was also a Certified Mentor with the Immigration and Customs Enforcement Mentoring Program, a Certified Instructor with the Federal Law Enforcement Training Center and a Supervising Attorney for the Litigation Clinical Placement Program with the University of Miami, St. Thomas University, Florida International University and Nova Southeastern University Schools of Law.

Her daily **Meg's Magical M.A.N.T.R.A.s** can be found on Instagram and Facebook @megnocero. She also blogs monthly *Inspirational Bliss*. Sign up for her newsletter at www.megnocero.com and get ready to *Sparkle & Shine*. She is a contributing writer for the collaboration entitled *Thrive Girl Thrive* released in August of 2019 and a contributing author for Amy Butler's book *Blossom: Create Love-Express Beauty-Be Kind* released in January 2016 in addition to her on-line magazine of the same name. Her *Butterflies & Bliss Trilogy* starting with *The Magical Guide to Bliss*, followed by *Sparkle & Shine* is completed in with her memoir entitled *Butterfly Awakens: A Memoir of Transformation Through Grief* published by She Writes Press.

In addition to being called on stage at the American Airlines Arena in Miami with Oprah Winfrey in 2014, appearing on CNN Español with Ismael Cala in 2016, and named *MizCEO* Entrepreneur of the Year in 2019, she hosts her own You Tube channel and a Podcast called *"Manifesting with Meg: Conversations with Extraordinary People."* She has been a guest on notable national and international podcasts and invited to speak to attorney and women groups with Royal Caribbean, AILA, the Florida Bar and the Attorney Wellness Exchange. She was also interviewed about her business, book and non-profit for on-line media such as MSNBC, CBS, Boston Herald, the Chicago Tribune and many more. Recently, she was invited to be on the "Improve Your Mind, Body, Soul and Even Your Wallet" panel at NY Book Expo/BookConline 2020 along with authors Raakhee

Mirchandani, and Bravo Celebrities Ryan Serhant and Bevy Smith.

Her first book, *The Magical Guide to Bliss* was named a Finalist in the Inspirational Non-Fiction Category for both the 2017 Next Generation Indie Book Awards, the 11th Annual National Indie Excellence Awards and won the 2019 Independent Press Award for Motivational Books.

Meg lives in Miami, Florida with her husband, wonderful children, and her amazing Tri-colored Shetland Sheepdogs. She values her family and friends. She loves her stationary bike - her riding meditation each day, Beachbody community, Peloton community, Yoga, and the movies. She is grateful for each and every day that she gets to follow her bliss.

www.megnocero.com

* * *

ALSO BY MEG NOCERO

The Magical Guide to Bliss

ILLUSTRATION BY KIM ANDERSON

https://www.instagram.com/kimartwork

kimartwork@yahoo.com

www.ingramcontent.com/pod-product-compliance
Lightning Source LLC
Chambersburg PA
CBHW041351290426

44108CB00001B/12